**HEALTH** REPORTS:
DISEASES AND DISORDERS

# DIABETES

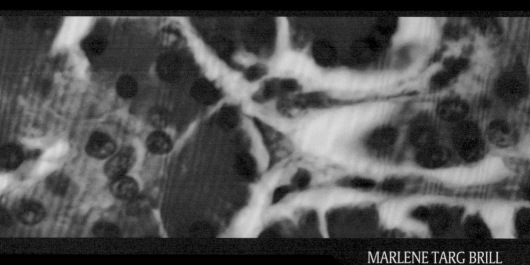

MARLENE TARG BRILL

 TWENTY-FIRST CENTURY BOOKS
MINNEAPOLIS

*Many people helped the author gather information and prepare this book. She wishes to thank the following people for their assistance: Marlene Davis, LCSW, clinical social worker specializing in chronic diseases; Dr. Ellen Rosenberg, psychologist; Christine Taylor, permissions, American Diabetes Association; Dr. William Thomas, pathologist; Dr. Amy Criego, pediatric endocrinologist, Park Nicollet Clinic; Dr. Meryl Abensohn; Michael Glazer; Sidney Medintz; Lauren Rosenberg; Doug Rosenberg; and Ralph von dem Hagen. A special thank-you goes to all the caring families who shared their stories so others can understand and help prevent diabetes.*

Twenty-First Century Books
A division of Lerner Publishing Group, Inc.
241 First Avenue North
Minneapolis, MN 55401 U.S.A.

Website address: www.lernerbooks.com

Library of Congress Cataloging-in-Publication Data

Brill, Marlene Targ.
        Diabetes / by Marlene Targ Brill.
            p.   cm. — (USA Today Health reports: Diseases and disorders)
        Includes bibliographical references and index.
        ISBN 978-0-7613-6085-8 (lib. bdg. : alk. paper)
        Diabetes—Juvenile literature. I. Title.
    RC660.5.B752 2012
    616.4'62—dc22                                                2010049454

Manufactured in the United States of America
1 – MG – 7/15/11

# CONTENTS

**USA TODAY**
**HEALTH** REPORTS:
DISEASES AND DISORDERS

JAN 1 1 2012

# CHAPTER ONE

# THE SUGAR DISEASE

*A*t birth, Brandy was a healthy, beautiful 9-pound (4-kilogram) baby girl. As she grew into a tall, strong toddler, she never even had a cold. Her parents rarely let her have candy, soda, or other sweet foods. Yet at four and a half years old, Brandy developed a lifelong disease involving sugar. Now she required constant supervision of her blood sugar, or blood glucose, and daily injections. Her parents often wondered what they did wrong.

*Jared was in seventh grade when his mother noticed that he ate and drank constantly. As a result, the increase in liquids made him urinate more often. The more Jared ate, the more he lost weight and felt tired. Jared never complained of feeling sick. So his mother thought he was a normal athletic thirteen-year-old. During a routine physical exam, the doctor asked Jared for a urine sample. Later, the nurse called Jared's mother. She asked that Jared return for a blood test the next morning before eating. The test showed high levels of sugar in Jared's blood. The doctor said Jared had diabetes. Jared and his mother were shocked.*

A diagnosis of diabetes can be overwhelming. Families wonder what diabetes is. They worry about what the disease means for the person who has it and their family. Finding answers to these questions offers the first step to understanding and managing diabetes.

## DIABETES BASICS

Diabetes occurs when the body cannot use sugar properly. The disease is marked by high levels of glucose. Glucose provides the energy needed to carry out daily activities. Usually, glucose enters the bloodstream from foods and drinks. Diabetes interferes with the way the body makes or uses the chemical insulin to regulate blood sugar.

Insulin is produced by the pancreas. This small organ lies behind the lower part of the stomach. In healthy individuals, insulin allows glucose to move from blood into the body's cells. Inside the cells, glucose is converted into energy. When cells cannot absorb glucose, sugar collects in the bloodstream or leaves the body in urine. Without sugar, the body loses energy, resulting in a host of symptoms.

Records dating as far back as 1500 B.C. describe symptoms of diabetes. Ancient Egyptian medical papers refer to a disease in which people "cannot stop either... drinking or making water." In the second century A.D., the Greek doctor Aretaeus noted that in some patients, "flesh and limbs melt into urine." Aretaeus named the condition "diabetes," from the Greek word for siphon, or passing through. The term referred to the way diabetes draws water from the body, similar to liquid moving through a siphon.

In a 1674 medical book on diabetes, English doctor Thomas Willis reported that his patients' urine "was wonderfully sweet as ... Honey or Sugar." Scientists debated the idea of sweet urine and its origins for years. In 1776 another British doctor, Matthew Dobson, conducted a different experiment. Dobson collected 2 quarts (1.9 liters) of urine from a patient who complained of excessive thirst, frequent urination, weakness, and cracked skin. Dobson heated the urine sample until all the liquid evaporated. What remained was a layer of white, sweet-smelling granules. In a bold move, he tasted the substance and confirmed that it tasted like sugar. Dobson reasoned that the sugar hadn't formed in the kidneys, as earlier doctors had proposed. Instead, Dobson argued that sugar in urine originated in the blood. Scientists still had no idea how sugar got into the bloodstream, what changes the sugar caused, or what to do about it. But Dobson's declaration linked diabetes to sugar in urine and blood. Later, doctors added the Latin term *mellitus*, or "honey sweet," to the term *diabetes* to describe the sweet taste.

# GLUCOSE AND INSULIN

Blood sugar is important because it serves as the body's main source of fuel for growth and activity. Glucose from food converts into energy during the process of digestion. When eating, the organs involved in digestion release chemicals that break down food into smaller, usable particles. The particles—including blood sugar—go to different parts of the body to help them function. Glucose enters the bloodstream and travels throughout the body. As it travels, blood sugar nourishes individual cells in muscles and tissues.

For cells to accept glucose, however, they must receive signals from hormones that aid digestion. Hormones are chemical messengers that travel in body fluids and stimulate cells to do their job. Hormones control many body processes, such as growth, sexual functions, and metabolism (the way the body chemically changes food into nutrients and energy). Glands and organs that produce hormones make up the endocrine system. These glands and organs release hormones directly into the bloodstream. Most hormones circulate throughout the body. But each hormone affects only a limited kind and number of cells.

The hormone insulin allows cells to receive glucose. Insulin is produced in the pancreas by clusters of cells called islets, or islets of Langerhans. Within the islets, beta cells manufacture insulin. Insulin acts as the gatekeeper that allows sugar into cells. The hormone helps regulate glucose levels in the bloodstream so just enough provides cells with fuel for energy. Throughout the day, blood glucose levels vary, depending on what you eat and how active you are. Too little glucose leaves the body without proper energy to function.

Other organs and chemicals also play roles in controlling glucose levels. The liver, an organ above the stomach, stores extra sugar for use in between meals and snacks.

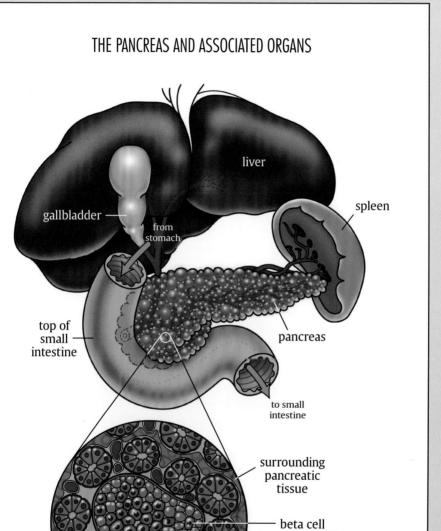

## THE PANCREAS AND ASSOCIATED ORGANS

liver

spleen

gallbladder

from stomach

top of small intestine

pancreas

to small intestine

surrounding pancreatic tissue

beta cell (secretes insulin)

islet

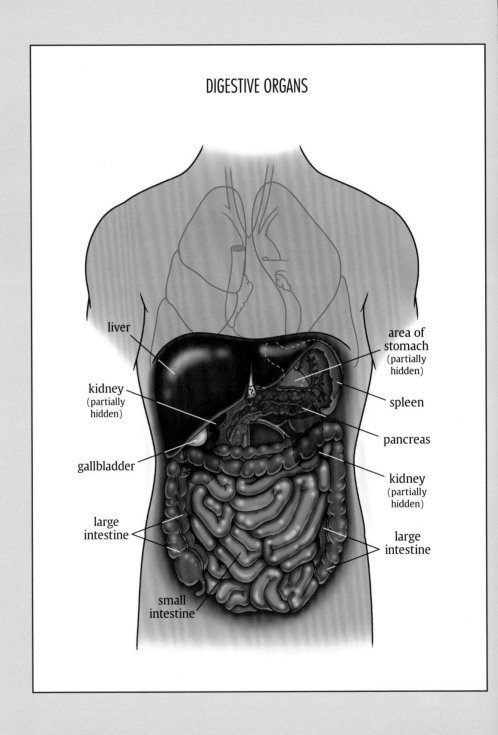

# DIGESTIVE ORGANS

liver

area of
stomach
(partially
hidden)

kidney
(partially
hidden)

spleen

pancreas

gallbladder

kidney
(partially
hidden)

large
intestine

large
intestine

small
intestine

When blood glucose levels drop and the body needs energy, the liver converts stored sugar—called glycogen—into glucose. The liver then releases the needed glycogen into the bloodstream. This process restores blood sugar levels to a healthy range.

Insulin and other hormones perform a balancing act to regulate blood sugar levels and provide fuel for cells. In healthy people, this process occurs automatically. Blood sugar levels stay within a set range. In people with diabetes, the body either cannot manufacture enough insulin or cannot use it properly. Glucose collects in the bloodstream instead of going into cells. Over time, high levels of blood sugar damage organs and body systems.

## SIGNS AND SYMPTOMS

Elevated levels or not enough sugar in the blood to fuel body cells can cause a range of diabetes symptoms. They may appear abruptly or gradually, depending on how well the body produces and uses insulin. Some types of diabetes can go undetected for years. With others, people know immediately that something is wrong.

The most common first signs of diabetes are excessive thirst and a need to urinate frequently. Jared likes to tell people that diabetes is the "drinking and peeing disease."

### INCREASED THIRST AND URINATION

Excess sugar draws water from body tissues. The sugary water is eliminated into urine. If urine contains too much sugar, the kidneys flush out extra water to make the urine less sugary. This creates even more urine, prompting extra trips to the bathroom. Excessive urination leads to increased thirst to replace the body's water supply. The cycle of drinking more liquids and urinating continues until the disease is detected and under control.

## FATIGUE

Without proper fuel, the body tires more easily. People with poorly controlled diabetes often have less energy than others their age. As a result, they might feel tired or irritable. They may perspire, tremble, or feel weak and confused. Sometimes diabetes causes symptoms similar to those of the flu.

## WEIGHT CHANGES AND INCREASED HUNGER

Without life-giving sugar, starved cells search to replace the necessary fuel. The need for fuel leads to increased appetite. Depending on the type of diabetes, some people gain weight from excessive eating to replace nutrients that leave the body. Others eat more food than usual and still lose weight. Without enough glucose for nourishment, their bodies burn fat for energy instead.

## BLURRED VISION

High blood sugar levels interfere with the balance of fluids in the eyes. Elevated glucose draws liquid from the eyes' lenses. In some people, this thins the lenses and contributes to problems with focusing. Over time, increased blood sugar may cause blood vessels in the eyes to weaken and bleed. Bleeding or leaking of fluid can damage vessels and trigger light flashes, spots, or halos around lights. Blurry vision from thinning lenses improves as blood sugar levels return to normal. But these and other vision problems require immediate attention from an eye doctor.

## HEALING DIFFICULTIES

Uncontrolled diabetes impairs the body's ability to battle germs and heal from infections, cuts, and bruises. People with diabetes face more frequent infections, such as in the bladder or skin. Their gums may become red, swollen, and tender. They may experience other dental and mouth problems as well.

## WHAT'S IN A NAME?

Many people with diabetes dislike being labeled "diabetic." They believe the term limits who they are and what they can accomplish. A better way to talk about diabetes is to put the person first, by saying "people with diabetes" or "a person who has diabetes." The term *diabetic* can be reserved to describe supplies or complications linked to the disease.

### OTHER SIGNS AND SYMPTOMS

Other signs and symptoms of diabetes may include:
- headache
- dry, itchy skin
- tingling feet and hands
- abdominal pain
- nausea
- vomiting

## A GROWING EPIDEMIC

In recent years, the number of people with diabetes worldwide has skyrocketed from 30 million to 230 million. The World Health Organization estimates that this number could reach 366 million by 2030. Cases in the U.S. alone approached 25.8 million in 2010, 2 million more than in 2007. Another 79 million tested with blood sugar levels high enough to be diagnosed with prediabetes. This term refers to people with an increased risk of developing the disease.

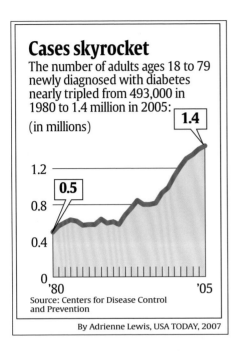

## Cases skyrocket

The number of adults ages 18 to 79 newly diagnosed with diabetes nearly tripled from 493,000 in 1980 to 1.4 million in 2005:

(in millions)

**1.4**

**0.5**

1.2

0.8

0.4

0

'80　　　　'05

Source: Centers for Disease Control and Prevention

By Adrienne Lewis, USA TODAY, 2007

Health officials fear that diabetes has become an epidemic. "Diabetes is this massive tidal wave hitting the country," said Dr. Aldo Rossini, from the University of Miami. The Centers for Disease Control and Prevention (CDC) projects that one in three U.S. children under the age five of will test with high sugar sometime during his or her lifetime.

This epidemic brings grave consequences. Diabetes is the seventh-deadliest illness in the United States. It can lead to heart disease, kidney disease, blindness, loss of limbs, and other serious problems that disrupt lives and are expensive to treat.

The medical community faces challenges in communicating the message about soaring rates of diabetes and what the diagnosis means. Many people with diabetes do not realize that high blood sugar can harm them, because they feel fine. Without concrete signs, newly diagnosed patients and those with prediabetes refuse to believe they are really sick. Yet early treatment remains important for preventing further damage. Changes in diet and activity, as well as medications, can help prevent or reduce complications of diabetes.

## LEARNING ABOUT DIABETES

Diabetes is a chronic, or lifelong, disease without a cure. Treatment requires individuals and families to make life-altering changes. A

**December 14, 2009**

From the Pages of USA TODAY

# Diabetes at a glance

23.6 million Estimated number of people in the United States who have diabetes

7.8% of the population who have diabetes

17.9 million Diagnosed cases

5.7 million Undiagnosed cases

57 million People with prediabetes, which puts them at risk for developing type 2 diabetes

**Other facts:**

Diabetes is the seventh-leading cause of death.

Diabetes is the leading cause of new cases of blindness among adults over 20.

Diabetes is the leading cause of kidney failure.

60% to 70% of people with diabetes have mild to severe forms of nervous-system damage.

Tens of thousands of limb amputations are done every year in people with diabetes.

*Source: American Diabetes Association*

valuable first step toward getting help is to learn how diabetes works, what signs to watch for, and how to keep sugar levels in check.

"You can't depend upon anyone else to find out what's right for your body," says Carl, aged fifty-eight, who has had sugar-related problems since he turned nineteen. "You need to read for yourself or explore on the Internet. Knowledge insures a healthier life."

# CHAPTER TWO

# TYPES OF DIABETES

Eleven-year-old Shawna was thirsty all the time. Because she drank a lot of liquids, she made frequent trips to the bathroom. After her twelfth birthday, Shawna's parents took her and a friend on a summer vacation. One day Shawna's friend watched in surprise as Shawna drank five large glasses of iced tea in one hour. Shawna looked weak. She said her eyes felt funny, and her mouth seemed dry. Her friend suggested that maybe Shawna had diabetes.

Back home, Shawna's mother took her to the doctor. He tested Shawna's blood and learned that she had type 1 diabetes. Her treatment involved testing her blood throughout the day and watching her diet. Because she had type 1 diabetes, Shawna also needed daily injections of insulin to replace what her body did not produce.

Jay was a successful computer technician and passionate gamer. He often got so involved in his work and computer games that he forgot to prepare healthy meals. For lunch he grabbed a burger to eat at his desk. For supper he'd pick up carry-out meals on his way home. Because Jay spent most of his time in front of the computer, he rarely exercised. Over the years, he steadily gained weight. By the time he turned forty years old, he was overweight.

Suddenly Jay dropped 20 pounds (9 kg) without trying. He felt thirsty all the time. Yet his eating and exercise habits never changed. Jay turned to his doctor for answers. She discovered that Jay had type 2 diabetes. She prescribed pills to lower his blood sugar. She also referred Jay to a nutritionist, a specialist in managing food choices. The nutritionist helped him learn to control his glucose levels by following a healthy diet and exercising regularly.

# ONE DISEASE: DIFFERENT TYPES

The term *diabetes* actually refers to a group of diseases. Each develops from a different cause but creates a problem with controlling blood sugar. Doctors determine which type of diabetes someone has based on the specific reason for the disease. The main forms of diabetes include type 1, type 2, and gestational, referring to blood sugar difficulties that begin when a woman is pregnant.

In the past, type 2 diabetes mainly targeted older, overweight people. Type 1 mostly began during the teen years. But doctors observed that older people can develop type 1 diabetes. The number of younger people with type 2 is increasing.

## TYPE 1 DIABETES

About 5 to 10 percent of all people with diabetes have type 1. In the United States, this means that more than a half million people have this form of the disease. With type 1 diabetes, the pancreas produces little or no insulin. Without this critical hormone, sugar stays in the bloodstream and cannot be used to fuel body cells. People with type 1 diabetes take insulin daily to ensure that sugar enters their cells and maintains healthy levels.

The disease generally begins in childhood or the teen years. But anyone can develop type 1 diabetes at any time. Because the disease affects more children and young adults, type 1 used to be called juvenile-onset diabetes, or insulin-dependent diabetes.

With type 1 diabetes, the body's immune system causes problems in the pancreas. A healthy immune system protects the body from disease and infection. When a foreign organism, such as bacteria or a virus, enters the body, the immune system sends an army of cells to flag and destroy the invader. Immune system proteins called antibodies help cells recognize and remember the foreign substance. Long-term cell memory fortifies the body against future invasion.

Sometimes the immune system produces a type of antibody called autoantibodies. Autoantibodies cannot distinguish between an intruder and the body's own cells. So autoantibodies mistakenly attack healthy cells. In the process, they destroy tissues and organs, causing a variety of diseases known as autoimmune diseases. In people with type 1 diabetes, the immune system attacks and destroys beta cells that produce insulin in the pancreas.

Scientists do not know exactly why the body's immune system attacks itself. Many researchers believe that some people inherit a tendency to develop type 1 diabetes. The disease process begins when something in the environment, such as a virus, triggers the disease. Illness stresses the body and requires more fuel from the cells for energy. In response, the pancreas rushes to produce more insulin to meet the demand for energy. When the demand for insulin increases, the body makes autoantibodies that destroy increasing amounts of beta cells. As the number of beta cells decrease, more symptoms of diabetes appear.

In a small number of cases, type 1 diabetes does not stem from an immune system problem. Researchers are investigating independent triggers in the environment, such as air pollution, specific viruses, medications, and food allergies that can cause type 1 diabetes. So far, scientists aren't sure what causes this form of the disease. But they are sure family history plays a role in most cases.

## TYPE 2 DIABETES

Type 2 is the most common form of diabetes, accounting for 90 to 95 percent of cases. Unlike type 1, type 2 diabetes is not an autoimmune disease. With type 2 diabetes, the pancreas usually continues to produce insulin. But for unknown reasons, beta cells either produce too little insulin or the body's muscle and fat cells no longer recognize insulin. Sometimes both occur to some degree.

# TYPE 1 AND TYPE 2 DIABETES

| | Age of Onset | Symptoms | Cause | Treatment |
|---|---|---|---|---|
| **Type 1** | Children/ teens | Appears suddenly | No or little insulin production | Insulin |
| **Type 2** | Adults/ some kids | Develops over years | Not enough insulin; cells resist insulin | Exercise, diet, pills, insulin |

Rejection of insulin is known as insulin resistance. When sugar cannot enter cells, it remains in the bloodstream. Dangerous amounts of sugar result in diabetes symptoms. While symptoms of type 1 diabetes usually appear abruptly, type 2 symptoms may emerge and progress slowly. Insulin resistance increases as production gradually decreases. As a result, type 2 diabetes can go undetected for years.

Scientists are unsure why cells resist insulin. They do know that excess weight and body fat contribute to developing this form of the disease. Being overweight forces the pancreas to work harder to manufacture extra insulin to balance sugar going into the cells. As demand for insulin rises, the pancreas loses its ability to produce enough. People who are overweight are more likely to have insulin resistance. Their excess fat interferes with the body's ability to use insulin.

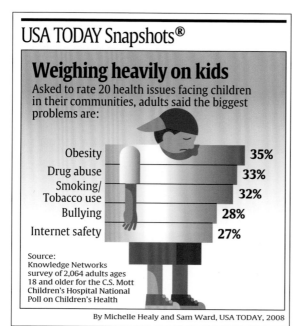

## USA TODAY Snapshots®

### Weighing heavily on kids

Asked to rate 20 health issues facing children in their communities, adults said the biggest problems are:

| | |
|---|---|
| Obesity | 35% |
| Drug abuse | 33% |
| Smoking/ Tobacco use | 32% |
| Bullying | 28% |
| Internet safety | 27% |

Source:
Knowledge Networks survey of 2,064 adults ages 18 and older for the C.S. Mott Children's Hospital National Poll on Children's Health

By Michelle Healy and Sam Ward, USA TODAY, 2008

Obesity is not the only cause of type 2 diabetes. About 10 percent of people with type 2 are not overweight. Scientists are investigating the role of family history and environmental factors in development of type 2 diabetes.

In the past, type 2 diabetes was known as adult onset diabetes because it typically occurred among middle-age or older adults. Since the 1990s, however, the numbers of children and adolescents with diabetes has increased dramatically. Doctors link this trend to a decrease in physical activity and increase in obesity. Children spend less time in physical activities, such as sports, recess, and outdoor play. They fill more time with watching television, playing video games, and messaging or working on computers. Typical diets include soda pop, chips, candy, and other sugary and high-fat foods. Lack of physical activity and eating too many unhealthy foods can lead to obesity, which contributes to type 2 diabetes. According to the CDC, one in three U.S. children born in 2000 will likely develop type 2 diabetes unless they exercise more and improve their diet.

Many people of all ages find they can reduce their risk of type 2 diabetes and control sugar levels by exercising more, eating better, and losing weight. Those with more severe diabetes may also need medication or insulin injections to manage their blood sugar levels.

## GESTATIONAL DIABETES

Gestational diabetes develops during pregnancy. About 3 to 8 percent of pregnant women develop this form of diabetes. Most often, the disease appears during the later months of pregnancy. At this time, changing hormone levels during pregnancy can increase insulin resistance. Hormones produced by the placenta, the organ carrying oxygen and nutrients to the unborn baby, cause the mother's body cells to resist insulin. As the placenta grows, it releases larger amounts of hormones. In some women, the pancreas cannot meet the added demand for insulin. The result is a condition similar to type 2 diabetes.

Often a woman with gestational diabetes experiences no obvious symptoms. Doctors usually find the problem after screening pregnant women for the disease with a blood test. If a woman tests positive for the disease, her doctor recommends a special diet. Should the diet fail to control sugar levels, the woman usually receives training to check her glucose levels and inject insulin.

At the same time, doctors monitor a woman's weight and the baby's movements to ensure a healthy delivery. Babies tend to grow larger in women who have uncontrolled diabetes. Large babies can be dangerous for the health of both mother and baby.

Gestational diabetes usually disappears after the baby is born. Hormones given off by the placenta drop to prepregnancy levels. But women with gestational diabetes have a 40 to 60 percent chance of developing type 2 diabetes in the next five to ten years. And babies have a higher risk of acquiring diabetes as they mature and grow.

USA TODAY Life SECTION D
www.usatoday.com

July 6, 2009

From the Pages of USA TODAY

# The dangers of diabetes

### Diabetes before pregnancy

- About one in 100 women have pregestational diabetes that occurs before they became pregnant.
- Women with poorly controlled pregestational diabetes are three to four times more likely to have babies with serious birth defects. Diabetes-related defects include heart, brain and spinal cord problems.
- Poorly controlled diabetes during early pregnancy can lead to miscarriage and stillbirth.
- Poorly controlled high blood sugar in pregnancy leads to large-birthweight babies. This causes risks during birth to mother and child.

### Gestational diabetes

- Gestational diabetes affects about 4% of all pregnant women. That's about 135,000 cases in the USA each year.
- Immediately after pregnancy, 5% to 10% of women with gestational diabetes are found to have diabetes, usually type 2.
- Women who have had gestational diabetes have a 40% to 60% chance of developing diabetes in the next five to ten years.
- Babies of women who have had gestational diabetes are at a higher risk of developing diabetes during their lives.

*Sources: March of Dimes, American Diabetes Association, Diabetes Care, Centers for Disease Control and Prevention, endocrinologist Sue Kirkman, The American College of Obstetricians and Gynecologists*

## OTHER TYPES OF DIABETES

Between 1 and 5 percent of diabetes cases do not fall into common categories. One rare form is maturity-onset diabetes of the young (MODY). This inherited condition affects children and teens and creates problems with producing enough insulin. Many people with MODY are normal weight, and their pancreas produces insulin, just not enough. People with MODY are often able to control their blood sugar levels with diet and exercise. If these recommendations fail, doctors prescribe insulin therapy. Injected insulin works better for MODY than medication, which helps with type 2 diabetes.

# RISK FACTORS

Unlike the flu or colds, diabetes cannot spread from one person to another. But certain factors increase the risk of developing diabetes, particularly type 2. Some risk factors, such as aging or ethnic background, cannot be avoided. But other factors involve lifestyle choices, such as lack of physical activity and excess weight, that can be controlled.

### FAMILY HISTORY

A key factor in developing the disease is family history. Individuals whose family members have type 1 or type 2 diabetes are more likely to develop the condition themselves. If a parent, a brother, or a sister has type 1 diabetes, a person's risk is fifteen times greater than for someone without a family history of type 1 diabetes. The link between family history and type 2 diabetes is strong but less clear.

Scientists continue to explore whether a defect in one or more genes contributes to the disease. Genes are basic units of heredity, the passing of traits from parents to offspring. Every human body contains trillions of cells. Each cell includes a set of rod-shaped chromosomes that contain many genes. Genes carry instructions for making proteins that perform most life functions. Genes ensure that the body grows, develops, and works properly. Genes determine physical characteristics, such as hair color, height, voice quality, and other traits.

Researchers discovered about eighteen genes that may raise the risk of developing type 1 diabetes. One set of genes targets specific antibodies and directs them to destroy healthy cells in the pancreas. Inheriting some or all of these genes increases the likelihood of developing type 1 diabetes. But scientists continue to explore how these genes interact with environmental factors to trigger the disease.

Researchers believe genes influence the onset of type 2 diabetes as well. So far, they have linked nine genes to type 2 diabetes. Some varieties of these genes lower the risk of type 2, while others increase the odds. Scientists have found that certain genes affect a person's weight. This is important because weight gain is a contributing factor for diabetes. Other genes play a role in how the pancreas manufactures insulin-producing cells. These genes may produce a protein that prevents cells from receiving insulin.

But studies with identical twins that have the same genes revealed that genes provide only part of the picture. If one twin develops type 1 diabetes, the other twin acquires the disease only 50 percent of the time. When one twin tests positive for type 2 diabetes, the other twin is at risk 70 percent of the time.

Researchers continue to study the role of conditions in the environment. Lack of exercise, poor diet, and weight gain can lead to type 1 and type 2 diabetes in addition to genetic makeup.

## GENDER AND ETHNIC BACKGROUND

Diabetes affects males and females equally and occurs in every nationality. But certain ethnic groups are more prone to the disease. For example, whites, especially from northern European countries, exhibit higher rates of type 1 diabetes than African Americans, American Indians, and Asians.

www.usatoday.com

USA TODAY

**Life**

SECTION D

June 22, 2009

From the Pages of USA TODAY

# Most type 2 diabetes can be stopped at childhood

When you're 8 years old, it can be hard not eating a cupcake when everyone else is having one. But that's the way life is for Nyla, a Philadelphia-area [in Pennsylvania] second-grader who was diagnosed with type 2 diabetes last year. She still gets treats now and then, but overall has to watch what she pops into her mouth.

An increasing number of children are being diagnosed with type 2 diabetes. Aggressive early treatment and lifestyle changes can help, and even snuff out disease symptoms. But more sweeping health care system changes, including better health insurance for older teens and people in their 20s, are required for young diabetics to age into healthy older adults, experts say.

There are various theories about why type 2 diabetes is appearing in greater numbers in the young now, says Melinda Sothern, professor of public health at Louisiana State University in New Orleans.

"We have a new generation of children who are metabolically different. We think there's been a series of genetic mutations—linked to environmental and life-style changes—over the last few generations that have led to this," says Sothern.

In Nyla's case, her father has diabetes, and Nyla is 25 pounds [11 kg] over-weight, says Martha Zeger, Nyla's doctor.

Nyla takes [the drug] metformin to lower blood sugar, and the family's health habits have been upgraded, say mom Stephanie. Macaroni and cheese has been replaced by whole grains, veggies, and proteins. Nyla swims competitively, too.

Ongoing support from a team of health experts, including a nutritionist, helps. But parents make the biggest difference," Zeger says.

Still, larger efforts, such as large-scale government programs at the preschool level, are needed to reverse the habits of a junk-food nation and curb the disease, Sothern says.

—*Mary Brophy Marcus*

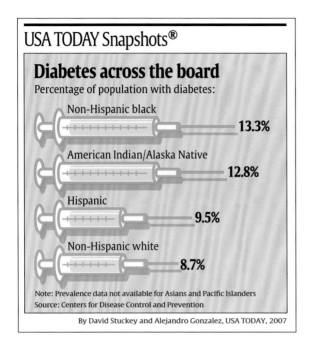

USA TODAY Snapshots®

**Diabetes across the board**

Percentage of population with diabetes:

Non-Hispanic black
**13.3%**

American Indian/Alaska Native
**12.8%**

Hispanic
**9.5%**

Non-Hispanic white
**8.7%**

Note: Prevalence data not available for Asians and Pacific Islanders
Source: Centers for Disease Control and Prevention

By David Stuckey and Alejandro Gonzalez, USA TODAY, 2007

In contrast, non-whites face a greater risk of developing type 2 diabetes than whites do. Compared with whites, African Americans encounter 1.8 times the risk of diabetes. Meanwhile, Hispanic groups experience 1.7 times and American Indians 2.2 times the risk. Asians of Far Eastern descent—including Chinese, Korean, and Japanese people—are particularly prone to type 2 diabetes. The threat is greater for recent immigrants to the United States.

One theory suggest that these immigrants might have led more physically demanding lifestyles and eaten lower-fat diets in their native countries. Once in the United States, they face a culture that encourages inactivity and a high-fat, sugar-laden diet. "When they give you the visa to the United States in Shanghai, Fujian or Beijing [China], they should stamp a clear warning: danger to your health," said Marcelo Suarez-Orozco, codirector of immigration studies at New York University.

## WEIGHT

Weight plays a more direct role in type 2 diabetes. Eight out of ten people with this form of the disease are overweight. One national study followed 122,000 women. Those who gained between 11 and 18 pounds (5 to 8 kg) over a fourteen-year period were nearly twice as likely to develop diabetes as women who gained less than 11 pounds during the same period. Women who gained between 24 and 44 pounds (11 to 20 kg) had five times the risk of developing diabetes.

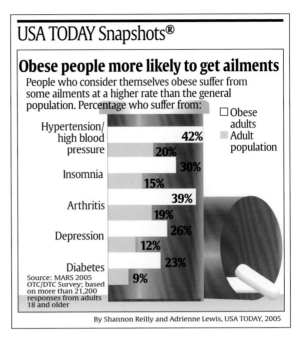

**USA TODAY Snapshots®**

**Obese people more likely to get ailments**

People who consider themselves obese suffer from some ailments at a higher rate than the general population. Percentage who suffer from:

☐ Obese adults
▨ Adult population

Hypertension/ high blood pressure — 42% / 20%
Insomnia — 30% / 15%
Arthritis — 39% / 19%
Depression — 26% / 12%
Diabetes — 23% / 9%

Source: MARS 2005 OTC/DTC Survey; based on more than 21,200 responses from adults 18 and older

By Shannon Reilly and Adrienne Lewis, USA TODAY, 2005

Being overweight increases the risk of diabetes. This is particularly true if the extra weight collects around the middle. Doctors call this shape an "apple" figure, rather than a "pear" figure with a flat stomach and fuller hips. Fat cells in the abdomen release fat into the bloodstream more easily than those elsewhere. Fat cells are less able than muscle cells to accept signals from insulin. This inability contributes to insulin resistance.

Another problem with excess weight occurs when fat cells collect in the liver. A healthy liver contains less than 5 percent of fat. A liver at risk of disease may comprise up to 50 percent fat. The higher amount makes the body resistant to its own insulin. Without the ability to regulate blood sugar, the body becomes open to type 2 diabetes. Studies indicate that about 30 percent of adults and children test with too much liver fat.

March 8, 2010

From the Pages of USA TODAY

# Inflammation and how it triggers illness

Researchers are beginning to understand the ways in which being overweight or obese contributes to a downward spiral of inflammation that can trigger heart disease, diabetes and other ailments.

Until about 10 or 15 years ago, doctors thought of fat as just fat, a bunch of cells that stored energy.

That changed in 1994, when researchers at Rockefeller University in New York discovered that fat cells actually produce leptin, a hormone that controls hunger and fat burning.

Suddenly, fat went from being a bunch of grease to an important player in the endocrine system. It's now known that fat produces at least 20 proteins, many of them hormones.

Then in 2005, a group at Columbia University in New York showed that when rodents were fed a high-fat diet or became obese, their fat tissues became inflamed. This launched a new effort to find the cause.

Normally, inflammation is healthy, a part of the body's fight against infections. But when it happens in response to obesity, it can contribute to numerous ills, such as type 2 diabetes.

The inflammation appears to happen because white blood cells that attack and eat infection congregate in fat tissue. A few years ago, the Columbia lab discovered that in lean people, only 5 percent of fat tissue is made up of white blood cells, while in the severely obese it can be more than 50 percent.

And why do they cause an immune response? One theory is that higher concentrations of fat could trigger white blood cells to go into inflammatory mode. When that happens, they shift from being simple eaters of dead cells to killers of foreign invaders. They carry signals between cells and can be used to attack and destroy infections.

—Elizabeth Weise

## LACK OF PHYSICAL ACTIVITY

Lack of physical activity adds to weight problems and an increased risk of type 2 diabetes. Exercise burns unused calories from food you eat and drink. When the body takes in more calories than it burns, the extra calories are stored as fat. The extra fat increases the chance of weight gain and diabetes.

Young people who spend much of their time looking at screens do so at the expense of physical activities. Many schools add to the problem of inactivity by cutting recess and physical education. As a result, many kids find fewer opportunities to exercise. Consequently, they face an increased risk of obesity and type 2 diabetes.

Lack of exercise and being overweight hits poorer families hardest. Families with lower incomes cannot afford time and money for fresh foods, programmed exercise, and regular health care available to wealthier households. Depressed income exposes families to higher risk of type 2 diabetes and lower levels of prevention and care for all types of diabetes.

## AGE

The threat of diabetes increases with age. As people grow older, their body systems work at a slower pace. This causes the body to burn fewer calories. Yet most people tend to eat the same amount and exercise less. Weight gain and loss of muscle mass increases the risk of type 2 diabetes. About one in four people over the age of sixty-five has type 2 diabetes.

## OTHER TRIGGERS

Several other factors raise the risk of blood sugar disease. Diabetes may develop following illness or use of medication that interrupts insulin production. Diabetes can result from infection; malnutrition; surgery; hydrocortisone drug treatment; and disorders of the pancreas, adrenal gland, and pituitary gland. Scientists continue to investigate the causes of diabetes. They try to educate the public about the dangers of this disease and healthy lifestyles that reduce the threat.

# CHAPTER THREE

# DETECTING DIABETES

*S*am was in his thirties when he was diagnosed with type 2 diabetes. In the 1940s, however, doctors rarely paid attention to high sugar levels unless patients reported symptoms. Sam watched his weight and stayed slim. But the doctor never told him to check his glucose levels or watch what he ate. By the age of seventy-four, Sam began to feel tingling in his legs. A new doctor determined that high blood sugar levels had damaged nerves in Sam's legs. This doctor prescribed drugs to control Sam's sugar levels. He taught Sam how to measure his blood sugar levels at home and which foods would help control these levels. By eating a balanced diet and taking medication, Sam learned to keep his sugar levels in a healthy range. He spent more time taking care of himself. But he believed the time was worth it to feel good and stay healthy.

Over time, high blood sugar levels can create major problems, harming organs throughout the body. The longer diabetes goes undetected, the more damage it can cause. Testing blood sugar as part of a regular checkup helps discover the disease early and begin treatment. Once a diagnosis is made, the goal is to keep blood sugar levels within a normal range as much as possible. This requires consistent self-testing of blood sugar.

## BLOOD SUGAR LEVELS

The body needs a certain amount of glucose in the bloodstream to fuel cells for energy. This amount varies throughout the day. It depends upon the type and amount of food eaten and the level of activity expended. Even with these changes, blood sugar levels usually stay within a narrow limit.

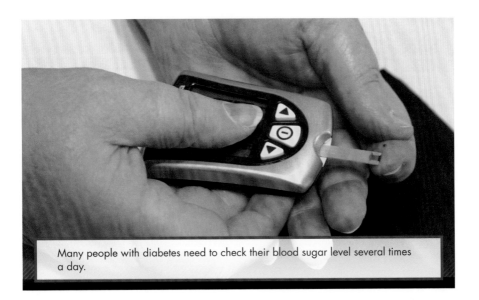

Many people with diabetes need to check their blood sugar level several times a day.

Normally, if you haven't eaten overnight, your glucose level the next morning measures between 70 to 100 milligrams per deciliter (mg/dl) of blood. That figure equals about 1 teaspoon of sugar per gallon (4 l) of water. Anything outside this range spells trouble. A blood glucose measurement higher than 100 mg/dl following an overnight fast signals hyperglycemia, or high blood sugar. Glucose levels below 70 mg/dl indicate hypoglycemia, or low blood sugar. Both extremes cause a variety of symptoms that, left untreated, can lead to serious illness or death.

## TESTING FOR DIABETES

Doctors identify and monitor diabetes through various tests that measure glucose levels in the blood.

### FASTING PLASMA GLUCOSE TEST

The fasting plasma glucose test is easy to perform and the most reliable. The patient does not eat or drink anything except water for eight to twelve hours before the test.

www.usatoday.com

USA TODAY

Life

SECTION D

February 22, 2000

From the Pages of USA TODAY

# Tests urged to fight diabetes' surge in obese kids

Physicians should start testing kids at high risk for type 2 diabetes—the type that normally strikes in adulthood—to combat an "emerging epidemic" of the disease among children, an expert panel says.

In the past, diabetic children nearly always had type 1. Type 2 usually strikes overweight adults over age 45. About 85% of type 2 cases in kids are linked to obesity, says panel chairman Arlan Rosenbloom of the University of Florida in Gainesville.

—Marilyn Elias

After this time period, a nurse or technician draws a blood sample from a vein in the patient's arm. A laboratory technician measures the amount of glucose in the blood plasma, the liquid part of the blood. Much like after a night's sleep, a normal glucose level after fasting is between 70 mg/dl and 100 mg/dl. If the test shows a level higher than 125 mg/dl, doctors suspect diabetes. They usually order a second fasting glucose test to confirm results before making a firm diagnosis of diabetes.

## RANDOM PLASMA GLUCOSE TEST

This test mirrors the fasting plasma test. But it measures blood sugar at any time and without a period of fasting first. A random test may be done as part of routine blood work during a physical exam with or without eating beforehand. If test results show glucose levels of 200 mg/dl or higher, doctors check further for diabetes. Most doctors request a fasting glucose test on another day to confirm the results.

## ORAL GLUCOSE TOLERANCE TEST

Doctors recommend the oral glucose tolerance test, also known as a glucose challenge test, less frequently. This test is more time-consuming, costly, and difficult to administer than a fasting blood sugar test. But doctors prefer the accuracy of the oral glucose test to detect gestational diabetes in pregnant women.

With an oral glucose test, the patient fasts for at least eight hours. After the fast, the patient first has blood drawn, then drinks 1 cup (0.3 liters) of very sweet liquid. The liquid contains 2.6 ounces (75 grams) of sugary-tasting glucose. This amount equals about three times the amount of sweetener in soft drinks. A technician measures blood sugar once an hour for the next three hours. Multiple test results show how the pancreas handles excess sugar over time. Glucose levels that rise or fall too much signal trouble. Glucose levels should rise quickly and then return to normal by the third hour. If not, the patient likely has diabetes.

## GLYCOSYLATED HEMOGLOBIN (A1C) TEST

This test is used to assess blood sugar control over a period of two to three months. It helps doctors and patients know how well treatment is working. A1C results show what percentage of hemoglobin—a protein in red blood cells—is sugarcoated. The goal for people with controlled blood sugar is less than 7 percent.

# PREDIABETES

Sometimes test results show glucose levels that are above normal but not high enough to qualify as diabetes. Borderline high blood sugar levels indicate prediabetes. The condition was once thought harmless, but doctors now know that having borderline blood sugar levels, or prediabetes, raises the risk of developing type 2 diabetes.

www.usatoday.com

USA TODAY

Life
SECTION D

February 2, 2009

From the Pages of USA TODAY

# Doctors use diabetes test as diagnostic tool

A test that doctors have been using for years to monitor blood sugar in people with diabetes may soon be recommended as a tool for diagnosing the disease.

Agreement among several leading diabetes organizations will lead to the publication of guidelines recommending the A1C test as a diagnostic tool for type 2 diabetes, says Matt Petersen of the American Diabetes Association [ADA].

The ADA guidelines currently recommend doctors use the fasting blood glucose (FBG) test in patients who are at risk for type 2 diabetes. A less common practice is for doctors to require an oral glucose tolerance test (OGTT).

Both are sensitive to measuring real-time glucose levels in the blood.

But results can be easily thrown off, for example, if a person has a cold or hasn't eaten properly. The benefit of the A1C test is that it can be taken at any time of day and is not thrown off by events of the day.

Also called the HbA1c or glycated [sugarcoated] hemoglobin test, it tells what your average blood glucose level was over the past two or three months by measuring the concentration of hemoglobin molecules in your red blood cells that have glucose attached to them.

So, if your A1C is an 8, that means 8% of your hemoglobin molecules are glycated. People who don't have diabetes typically have about a 6 or less reading. Higher results may indicate diabetes.

—Mary Brophy Marcus

A diagnosis of prediabetes, also called glucose impairment, may be based on results from either the fasting glucose or oral glucose tolerance test. Impaired fasting glucose (IFG) means blood sugar levels test between 100 and 125 mg/dl after fasting overnight. Impaired glucose tolerance (IGT) refers to glucose levels between 140 and 199 mg/dl after two hours during the oral glucose tolerance test.

The U.S. government estimates that 40 percent of Americans ages forty to seventy-four test in the prediabetic range. That's about 41 million people, a very large number of Americans. Many of these adults will develop type 2 diabetes within the next ten years. By then, they probably will experience diabetes-related problems, such as diseases of the heart, blood pressure, and eyes.

People with prediabetes can take action to prevent full-blown diabetes from developing. The most important steps involve losing weight, choosing healthier foods, and exercising regularly. According to the National Institute of Diabetes and Digestive and Kidney Diseases, the risk of diabetes drops after losing 5 to 7 percent of body weight through diet and increased physical activity. In one study, three thousand people with impaired glucose tolerance lost 10 to 14 pounds (5 to 6 kg) and walked at least thirty minutes each day for five days a week. They reduced their risk of diabetes by almost 60 percent. Another group in the same study took medication but did not follow the diet and exercise program. Results for this group revealed only half the success (31 percent reduced risk). These studies bring hope to the medical community that individuals can influence control of their blood sugar levels.

## THE DIABETES CARE TEAM

After learning of high blood sugar, patients need to gather information. People with diabetes have a lot to learn about their disease and treatment. Anyone with such a serious, long-term disease may want support to help manage their condition and stick with a treatment plan. They can benefit from regular visits to their family doctor as well as various specialists. These are physicians who concentrate on a particular area of medicine, such as feet or eye health. In some cities, doctors send newly diagnosed patients to training sessions at a hospital

www.usatoday.com
USA TODAY
Life
SECTION D

**March 28, 2002**

From the Pages of USA TODAY

# Medical experts warn of the dangers of 'prediabetes'

Medical experts from the Department of Health and Human Services, Centers for Disease Control and Prevention, National Institutes of Health, and American Diabetes Association issued guidelines for diabetes screening and the first recommendations for treating prediabetes.

Recommendations include:
- People at high risk for diabetes should become aware of the benefits of modest weight loss and physical activity.
- People age 45 or older are candidates for screening to detect impaired fasting glucose or impaired glucose tolerance, especially those with a body mass index (BMI) [a measurement of muscle, bone, and other nonfat tissue] of 25 or higher, or those under 45 with a BMI 25 or higher and one other risk factor (family history, gestational diabetes, nonwhite, hypertension [high blood pressure], or high cholesterol).
- Patients with impaired glucose tolerance or impaired fasting glucose should be given counseling on weight loss and increasing exercise. Follow-up counseling is important and monitoring for diabetes should be performed every one to two years.

—*Anita Manning*

or clinic. In these classes, people with diabetes meet several health-care professionals who help them take charge of their treatment and overall health. This group becomes their diabetes care team, professionals they can count on for guidance and support.

## ENDOCRINOLOGIST

An endocrinologist is a medical doctor trained to identify and treat disorders of the endocrine system. The endocrine system includes glands and organs that secrete hormones into the bloodstream. One of these glands is the pancreas, which produces insulin. Endocrinologists test for diabetes, determine the type and extent of the disease, and recommend treatment. Children and adolescents with diabetes see a pediatric endocrinologist, an endocrinologist who treats young people.

## DIABETES EDUCATOR

A diabetes educator explains what diabetes is and answers questions about living with the disease. Diabetes educators train patients to monitor their blood sugar with a blood sugar meter. They help patients establish a routine for checking blood sugar levels regularly. And they teach patients to watch for symptoms of high or low blood sugar. For people who take insulin, a diabetes educator shows them how to inject the drug and adjust doses.

Diabetes educators usually are registered nurses, dietitians, or pharmacists who receive special training in the disease. They see patients in doctor's offices, hospitals, or clinics. "I went to the hospital for a couple days, and the diabetes educator gave me a thorough grounding in what diabetes is and how to manage it," Jared says.

Diabetes educators can help new patients deal with their diagnosis.

### DIETITIAN OR NUTRITIONIST

Dietitians, or nutritionists, teach patients how to control their blood sugar and weight through diet. They work with patients to plan a balanced diet they feel comfortable following. A dietitian provides information about measuring portion sizes and balancing amounts of nutrients in meals.

Patients with diabetes often work with a variety of doctors, such as podiatrists, or foot doctors.

"The dietitian talked about maintaining a healthy diet," Shawna remembers. "In the beginning, I was a lot stricter with following my diet. After a while, I learned to estimate food and insulin amounts."

### OTHER SPECIALISTS

Because high blood sugar affects various organs, people with diabetes often see several different doctors regularly. Ophthalmologists examine eyes to prevent diabetes-related vision problems. Podiatrists, or foot doctors, check feet for poor blood circulation and sores that can lead to infection. Foot doctors teach patients how to safely trim their toenails and deal with corns and calluses. People with diabetes may see a dermatologist, or skin doctor, to treat skin infections. And they visit the dentist regularly to help them prevent mouth-related problems.

## LEADING THE DIABETES CARE TEAM

In the end, the patient is the most important person on the care team. If you have diabetes, even as a young person, it's up to you to take charge of your treatment. You are the team leader.

As leader, your first step is to admit you have a chronic illness that will require lifelong attention. Next, you must be willing to follow your treatment program. This usually means adapting diet and physical activities as your disease changes. You can get help, support, and guidance from a diabetes care team or through agencies, such as the American Diabetes Association. But controlling blood sugar is a personal journey, one guided by the person with the condition.

# CHAPTER FOUR

# TAKING CONTROL

Jim is a retired doctor who has type 2 diabetes. He wants to avoid complications from the disease, so he watches his blood sugar levels carefully. Jim tests his blood every morning and two hours after he eats. His blood sugar meter shows the date, the time, and the blood sugar measurement. He records these figures in a log to take to his doctor.

Jim also follows a meal plan that emphasizes whole grains, vegetables, lean sources of protein, and fruits. He walks an hour most days. Healthy eating, an activity plan, and regular visits with a health-care team keep Jim's diabetes from getting worse.

## TREATMENT BASICS

In the past, having diabetes guaranteed a shortened life. That's because uncontrolled blood sugar levels contribute to a host of other problems. Uncontrolled blood sugar contributes to high blood pressure (the force of blood against artery walls), heart disease, kidney failure, blindness, loss of limbs, and nerve damage. But advances in diabetes care have improved the outlook for people with diabetes. Patients who balance their sugar levels can expect to live long, healthy, and active lives.

"Treatment has changed a lot since 1993 when Jared was diagnosed," says his mother, Ann. "There are new meters for measuring blood sugar and long-acting and short-acting insulin. With tight control of blood sugar, people with diabetes can help stave off problems."

The main focus of treatment is to keep blood glucose levels within a normal range. Controlled levels are key to preventing symptoms and complications. To maintain healthy blood sugar levels, patients must follow a multipronged plan. Learning what to do and staying on course can be challenging. Many people rely on a diabetes care team, peer support group, or online support group to help them adjust to lifestyle changes diabetes requires. The mainstays of treatment include a healthy diet, weight control, physical activity, and regular blood glucose testing.

Salads and other green vegetables are important to a healthy diet.

## CHOOSING FOODS

Food you eat contributes to your overall health. You acquire energy and vitamins and minerals by eating a mix of carbohydrates, proteins, and fats. Dietitians recommend a diet that includes a variety of foods offering a healthy balance of nutrients. This is true whether or not you have high blood sugar levels. But food selection, portion size, and timing of meals become more important if you have diabetes. What you eat, how much you eat, and when you eat all affect glucose levels.

At one time, doctors told patients with diabetes to stop eating all sweets and follow a prescribed diet. Popular thinking assumed that eating sugary snacks made glucose levels rise higher and quicker than other foods. Worried patients feared that diabetes sentenced them to a lifetime of boring food and limited choices.

More recently, scientists have discovered that a person's reaction to different foods depends on several factors. Does one food, even within the same food group, cause blood sugar levels to spike more than another? How large a portion triggers a reaction? Was the sugary food eaten in combination with other foods? All these elements go into planning a healthy diet for someone with sugar problems.

## MAKING SENSE OF CARBS

Carbohydrates, or carbs, supply the body's main source of fuel for energy. The body breaks down these foods into sugar that cells can use. Dietitians classify carbohydrates as simple or complex according to how quickly the body digests and absorbs the sugars they contain.

Simple carbohydrates are made up of one or two types of sugars. These absorb in the body quickly, often making blood sugar rise faster. Simple carbohydrates are found in fruits, milk products, and foods made with processed and refined sugars. Processed foods include those made from white flour, such as pasta and breads. Refined sugars are used in sweets, such as candy, table sugar, cake, and cookies, and nondiet beverages.

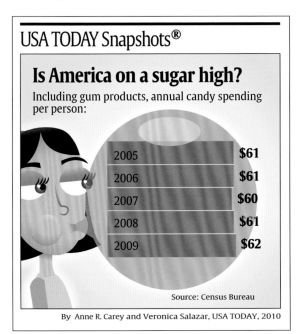

USA TODAY Snapshots®

**Is America on a sugar high?**

Including gum products, annual candy spending per person:

|  |  |
|------|--------|
| 2005 | $61 |
| 2006 | $61 |
| 2007 | $60 |
| 2008 | $61 |
| 2009 | $62 |

Source: Census Bureau

By Anne R. Carey and Veronica Salazar, USA TODAY, 2010

Complex carbohydrates contain three or more sugars. The body is able to absorb these slower than simple carbohydrates. Complex carbohydrates form the basis of whole-grain products, including whole-wheat bread, oatmeal, and brown rice. They are found in beans, peas, legumes, and other starchy vegetables, such as potatoes and corn.

Nonstarchy vegetables, such as broccoli, celery, zucchini, and carrots, are complex carbohydrates that are mostly fiber. Fiber comes from cells of plant walls that stay largely undigested in the human digestive system. Examples of fibrous foods include oatmeal, beans, and fresh vegetables. Because fibrous foods remain mostly undigested, they take longer to travel through the digestive system. The result from eating them is a slower rise in blood glucose than from eating foods consisting of simple carbohydrates.

As an added bonus, complex carbohydrates and high-fiber foods make a person feel full more quickly and for longer. These foods contain many important vitamins and minerals. Complex carbohydrates provide excellent nutrition naturally. In contrast, refined sugars, such as candy, lack vitamins, minerals, and fiber. Refined sugars are often referred to as empty calories because they have little or no nutritional value. But they do have calories that contribute to weight gain.

People with diabetes find they maintain better control of blood sugar by eating a variety of complex carbohydrates and fiber-rich foods. In one study, participants reduced their blood sugar levels by about 10 percent by increasing their intake of high-fiber foods. Based on this and other studies, dietitians recommend a diet rich in fibrous foods to stabilize blood sugar levels. Nutrition experts advise that between 40 and 60 percent of daily calories come from carbohydrates.

## CARB COUNTING

Doctors often suggest counting carbohydrates as one way to plan meals. Counting carbs helps maintain good blood sugar control and determine how much insulin to take. One carb serving is equal to 15 grams of carbohydrates. Several booklets or websites offer listings of carb counts for various foods. Or you can read the nutrition facts label on food packages.

When you read food labels, focus on total carbohydrates and serving size. For example, one-half cup of bran cereal may contain 23 total carbohydrates. Think about how many servings to eat. Decide whether you would add milk, sugar, or fruit. Then add the total amount of carbs for everything.

Reading labels and checking on total carbohydrates and serving size are important when shopping for healthy food.

Insulin users count carbs to determine their insulin dose for a meal. For those who do not require insulin, counting carbohydrates provides one way to calculate how many servings are in a meal or snack. This number helps you keep the day's eating in balance. Carb counting may seem daunting at first. But learning average carbs per food becomes second nature with practice.

## ADDING PROTEINS AND FATS

Combining carbohydrates with proteins and fats, the two other main food groups, helps control sugar levels. Proteins include meat, poultry, seafood, eggs, nuts, beans, soy products, and legumes. The body uses proteins to build and repair tissues. Eating protein-rich foods with carbohydrates causes blood glucose levels to rise more slowly than eating carbs alone.

Protein-rich foods are important for a healthy, balanced diet. But too much protein can contribute to kidney problems and weight gain from excess calories. Dietitians suggest that between 10 and 20 percent of your total daily calories contain proteins.

Fats are found in animal products, such as meat, fish, dairy products, and plant foods, such as nuts, avocados, and olives. Fats have gotten a bad reputation from low-fat fad diets and manufacturers trying to sell low-fat products. But the body needs fat as a source of stored energy. Without some fat in the diet, your body burns tissue and muscle for food. Yet eating too much fat or too much of the wrong kind of fat increases the likelihood of weight gain. And excess weight can lead to type 2 diabetes and other serious health issues.

Health professionals recommend that no more than 30 percent of total calories each day come from fats. Less than one-third of these fat calories should be from animals, such as meat and dairy. Healthier sources of fat are found in fish and fish oils, seeds and nuts, and vegetable oils, such as canola, olive, and soybean oils.

# HOW MANY CALORIES DO YOU NEED?

Calories are a measurement of energy produced from food that the body uses. Most energy from food is released as heat to control body temperature. A calorie is a measure of that heat. Carbohydrates, proteins, and fats each produce different amounts of energy, or calories. Fats have 9 calories per gram. Proteins and carbohydrates each have 4 calories per gram.

If you consume more calories than you burn, your body stores the unused calories as fat. That's why it's important to eat within the recommended number of calories each day. Daily calorie guidelines established by the U.S. Department of Agriculture vary according to age and activity level.

| | |
|---|---|
| Children ages 2–6 | 1,600 calories per day |
| Inactive women | 1,600 calories per day |
| Older adults | 1,600 calories per day |
| Children ages 7–12 | 2,200 calories per day |
| Teenage girls | 2,200 calories per day |
| Active women | 2,200 calories per day |
| Inactive men | 2,200 calories per day |
| Teenage boys | 2,800 calories per day |
| Active men | 2,800 calories per day |

## CREATING A MEAL PLAN

Many people with diabetes find it helpful to follow a meal plan. A plan follows a set of guidelines for eating a variety of foods. Within these guidelines, you can choose your favorite foods and decide portions to eat.

Every meal plan is different. For example, people who are overweight may want a plan that includes meals and snacks throughout the day but provides fewer calories overall. But insulin users must balance food choices and timing with amounts of insulin and activity.

"I became more aware of what I ate and how it affected me after learning I had diabetes," says Emily, Jared's younger sister, who also has diabetes. "I've been to a dietitian several times, and we adjust my meal plan. It helps to have a meal plan because then I know how much insulin to take."

A meal plan begins with keeping a log of everything you eat and any reactions these foods cause. A log helps people with diabetes and their dietitian choose foods and mealtimes that ensure stable blood glucose levels. Some people with diabetes can eat three meals a day without snacking and keep their blood sugar levels under control. Others require several smaller meals and snacks between meals. A complete log helps determine correct portion sizes and the healthiest balance of carbohydrates, proteins, and fats to eat.

**USA TODAY Snapshots®**

**Fast-food buyers**

Adults younger than 35 spend the most each week on fast food:

Amount spent each week

$35 — 24 and under
$44 — 25-34
$33 — 35-44
$25 — 45-54
$18 — 55 and older

Source: Greenfield Online survey of 1,000 adults for Jenny Craig. Margin of error ±3% percentage points.

By Michelle Healy and Julie Snider, USA TODAY, 2009

# CREATE YOUR PLATE

The American Diabetes Association created an easy way to figure out the types and portions of foods to eat at each meal. The organization calls it Create Your Plate. The association suggests picturing each meal as a dinner plate divided into halves, with one half split into two sections:

- One-fourth of the plate has complex carbohydrates including grains or starchy foods, such as rice, pasta, potatoes, beans, or corn.

- One-fourth holds proteins, such as meat, fish, poultry, meat substitute, or tofu.

- One-half is covered with salads or nonstarchy vegetables, such as lettuce, tomatoes, broccoli, cucumbers, cauliflower, green and red peppers, and artichokes.

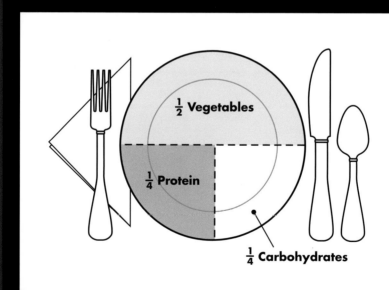

One of the most difficult parts of meal planning is deciding portion size. The United States subscribes to a supersize culture where "more is better." This mindset has led to gigantic serving sizes in restaurants and packaged food. Portions have doubled or tripled in recent years. Many Americans have grown accustomed to these large servings. But large portions pack added calories that contribute to weight gain and soaring blood sugar levels. Choosing smaller serving sizes helps with weight loss and diabetes management.

## FOOD EXCHANGES

Food exchanges offer another option, much like carb counting, for helping people choose healthier foods. Exchanges divide food choices into categories: vegetables, fruits, fats, milk products, and meats or meat substitutes. The plan allows for a given number of servings or choices from each food group at every meal. The number of servings from a given group depends on individual goals for limiting calories or carbohydrates and providing a nutritional balance.

The choices within each food group are called exchanges. Each choice, or exchange, provides similar nutrients and effects on blood sugar as another choice in the same category. The idea that one food can be exchanged for another helps with planning varied, yet healthy meals. The American Diabetes Association produces materials that identify exchanges for meal planning.

## WATCHING WHAT YOU EAT

Preparing and implementing a meal plan can be puzzling. People with—and without—diabetes may find these other suggestions to make healthier food choices helpful.

## READ FOOD LABELS

One of the best ways to improve your health is to read the labels on food packages. Federal guidelines require companies to disclose nutrition information on most food packages and on menus at restaurant chains with more than 20 outlets. Nutrition facts usually include the amount of calories, carbohydrates, fats, proteins, and fiber in an item. Many labels give percentages of daily vitamin requirements one portion meets.

Equally important, nutrition labels list the product's ingredients. Manufacturers list ingredients according to weight. So those listed first count for the bulk of the product. Similarly, ingredients at the end of the list represent the smallest proportion of the item.

Nutrition facts help people with diabetes decide which foods and in what amounts fit into their overall program. Labels describe what manufacturers calculate as a single portion size, which can help with meal planning. But keep in mind that stated portion sizes may differ from exchange serving sizes or healthy portions for a particular meal plan.

## EAT COLORFUL FOODS

Another tool to help you make healthier choices involves eating a variety of colorful foods. A colorful plate displays an array of fruits, vegetables, grains, dairy products, and meats. Brightly colored fruits and vegetables—apples, broccoli, squash, eggplant, blueberries, and peppers—help keep blood sugar highs and lows in check.

In one study of people with type 2 diabetes, half the participants ate a vegan diet, which centers on fruits, vegetables, beans, and grains. They omitted meats, added fats, and dairy products. The other half of participants followed a diet that included small amounts of animal products. Results showed that 43 percent of participants on the vegan diet reduced their doses of diabetes medication.

December 14, 2009

From the Pages of USA TODAY

# Armstrong has a new passion: Diabetes

Anyone who has heard of him—and millions have—knows Lance Armstrong is all about cancer advocacy. Now the seven-time Tour de France winner and cancer survivor is directing his star power and reputation for vitality at another disease: diabetes.

Armstrong introduced a feature called MyPlate D on his popular website, Livestrong.com. It is an extension of Livestrong.com's current tool that let users track food intake and exercise. The website encourages visitors to communicate with others who have similar health and fitness objectives.

MyPlate D was developed for people who have type 2 diabetes to help them break food down to its nutritional components beyond just calories to include carbohydrates, fats, proteins, and sodium. It also lets people track insulin use and monitor glucose.

"Users will start to recognize trends in their diet that may lead to spikes in glucose levels and be able to change their daily habits," says registered dietitian Alyse Levine, nutrition consultant for Livestrong.com who helped develop MyPlate D. "The site is free and is the

Lance Armstrong, shown here before a race in 2011, has used his website to help people with diabetes make healthy food choices.

largest food and fitness database online."

"Much like with cancer survivors, people with diabetes have been dealt this hand, a health challenge," Armstrong says. "Ultimately, we wanted to help them achieve a healthy quality of life, help them live to their fullest."

—*Mary Brophy Marcus*

# DO THE MATH

People in good control of their diabetes do a lot of math. For example, say that the serving size on a nutrition label shows that five pieces of the food total 22 grams of carbohydrate per serving. Someone with diabetes needs to calculate the number of pieces in a standard 15-gram serving size on their meal plan. The answer is between three pieces, or 13.2 grams, and four pieces, or 17.6 grams. Ten pieces, or 44 grams, are three servings.

Consumers also need to pay attention to health claims on food packaging. Food manufacturers sometimes pay for claims from health-related organizations to print on packages. Or manufacturers make misleading statements about a food's nutritional value. The best way to understand what you're buying and eating is to read the nutrition facts panel carefully.

Only 26 percent of participants on the other diet reduced their medication. Moreover, the vegan group doubled their weight loss— 14 pounds (6 kg) compared with 7 pounds (3 kg). And they tested with more stable blood sugar levels.

## CHOOSE WATER-DENSE FOODS

Another tip for a healthier diet is to eat foods loaded with water. Water-logged foods include fruits, vegetables, and cooked whole grains. Foods with a high water content pack fewer calories into larger quantities. The result is you can eat more and feel full with fewer calories. The full feeling comes from water and fiber that fill your stomach quicker. A full stomach suppresses appetite and helps with weight loss and blood sugar control.

## AVOID ALCOHOL

Drinking alcohol often spells trouble for people with diabetes. Alcohol can cause blood sugar levels to drop or rise, depending on the individual and type of drink. Combining alcohol with medication that lowers blood sugar levels may cause hypoglycemia.

If adults with diabetes choose to drink, they should do so in moderation. Equally important, the type of alcoholic beverage makes a big difference in how the body reacts. Sugary drinks, such as sweet wines, wine coolers, and alcohol mixed with juices, contain higher amounts of sugar and carbohydrates. These may increase blood glucose levels too much and too quickly. Another way to keep glucose levels in check is to eat before and while drinking. Food absorbs and balances some effects of the alcohol.

## KEEP MOVING

"Diabetes can be helped by lifestyle choices. It makes you take charge of your lifestyle and be extra healthy to cope with it effectively," Jared says. "I exercise. I ride my bicycle a lot. I play basketball. I do yoga. I jog."

Physical exercise helps prevent and control diabetes. Exercise promotes weight loss and aids the body in converting sugar to fuel. In addition, people who stay physically active enjoy better health and well-being overall. A boost in physical activity of any kind translates into more energy; longer life; and less risk of illness (including heart disease, high blood pressure, and osteoporosis, a bone disease).

When you exercise, your muscles contract (tighten) and relax. To do this, they use glucose from the bloodstream for energy. At the same time, moderate prolonged activity, such as swimming or jogging, signals the liver to release glycogen into the bloodstream. The glycogen makes cells more sensitive to insulin. As the body uses glycogen for energy, blood sugar levels fall. The stabilizing effect

Regular exercise, such as tennis, helps people with diabetes stay healthy. Exercising can reduce the risk of developing type 2 diabetes.

continues for hours after physical activity.

A regular exercise program gives people a powerful tool for man aging their own health and well-being. According to Dr. Richard K. Bernstein, author of *Dr. Bernstein's Diabetes Solution*, "Type 1 diabetics who engage in a regular exercise program tend to take better care of their blood sugars and diet." For people with type 2 diabetes, exercise contributes to better glucose control and a reduced need for medication or insulin. For those with prediabetes, exercise decreases the likelihood of developing type 2 diabetes.

The American Diabetes Association recommends exercising for thirty to sixty minutes most days each week. Find one or more activities that are fun or satisfying enough to hold your interest over time. Your choice of activity need not be strenuous. The best blood sugar control results from extended, moderate activity. Be sure to wear comfortable footwear and polyester or cotton-polyester socks to prevent blisters and keep your feet dry. In hot weather, drink water before and during exercise. Because exercise affects blood sugar levels, ask your diabetes care team about when to check your blood sugar. Coordinate your insulin or medication with the physical activity.

www.usatoday.com

USA TODAY

Life
SECTION D

**December 22, 2008**

From the Pages of USA TODAY

# QB keeps type 1 diabetes in check, stays on his game

Jay Cutler has a cannon for an arm. You'd never know that the quarterback for the Denver Broncos spends a good portion of every game on the sidelines keeping tabs on his type 1 diabetes, a condition, that if left unmonitored, can cause severe health problems.

Cutler, who was diagnosed just before his 25th birthday, uses a fingerprick kit to check his blood sugar levels, sometimes half a dozen times during a game. If the reading is too low, he gulps down enough Gatorade to push it up. His medication is always on hand in case his blood sugar jets abnormally high.

Being an athlete with type 1 has its complexities, but research shows exercise improves the health of patients with diabetes, says Michael Jensen, professor of medicine at the Mayo Clinic.

Snacking, hydrating [getting enough liquids], and protecting vulnerable body parts become lifelines for athletes with diabetes. But Cutler and experts say the condition doesn't have to stop a person from becoming a star athlete—or even enjoying a game of flag football now and again.

"When you and I exercise for any period of time, whether it's light or hard, our body needs less insulin. The pancreas

With the Chicago Bears since 2009, quarterback Jay Cutler gets ready to throw a pass in a game in 2011. Cutler closely monitors his type 1 diabetes to stay healthy while playing.

automatically does that for us," Jensen says. With type 1 diabetes, that doesn't happen naturally. Blood sugar can drop super-low during sports, and the only way to correct it is with food. If it jumps too high, Jensen says, insulin is needed.

Type 1 athletes should know their bodies and what's right for their sports routine, Jensen says. "It varies immensely depending on the sport you're in."

*—Mary Brophy Marcus*

# GETTING ENOUGH SLEEP

About six in ten people admit they don't get enough sleep on a regular basis. Recent studies have shown that sleep plays a role in overall health and well-being. Sleep-deprived people are more apt to grab sweets for energy and to keep themselves alert. This habit can lead to overweight, which puts the sleep-deprived at greater risk for obesity, heart disease, and diabetes. For people who already have diabetes, getting enough sleep plays a role in balancing blood glucose levels and maintaining a healthy weight.

# MONITORING BLOOD SUGAR

Diabetes interferes with the body's natural ability to identify and regulate blood sugar levels. The only way to know if blood sugar levels are within a safe range is to check them regularly. Therefore, patients must monitor their glucose levels with a meter. Monitoring helps guide treatment plans and decisions about medication, diet, and activity.

## DRAWING BLOOD SAMPLES

Blood glucose testing relies on measuring samples of blood. A variety of blood sugar meters are available. Most read plasma in a drop of blood.

To get the blood sample, you use a lancet to prick the side of your finger. A lancet is a sharp, fine needle. Lancets come in spring-loaded devices that look like pens. They are easy to use and cause little pain. Some meters allow you to draw blood from a site other than the finger, such as your palm or forearm. Other blood glucose meters also serve as insulin injection pens.

In the early twenty-first century, scientists created a newer testing device called a continuous glucose monitor (CGM). The CGM measures glucose levels in interstitial fluid. This is the clear fluid under the skin that carries glucose and other nutrients through the bloodstream to cells. Some continuous monitors use a tiny sensor inserted beneath the skin. The sensor transmits blood glucose information to a monitor worn on a belt or in a pocket. The sensor can stay under the skin for up to three days before it must be replaced. Another device worn on top of the skin is a continuous glucose monitoring patch.

Most continuous blood glucose monitors measure levels every few minutes. Frequent reports alert users whether their levels are heading up or down. Some monitors sound an alarm when blood sugar goes too high or too low. The vital information warns you to eat a snack or stop exercising to correct a dangerously low blood sugar level. To prevent a damaging high, you may choose to exercise or reduce the carbohydrate count of the next meal.

This kindergartner wears a blood glucose monitor to keep track of her blood sugar levels at all times.

www.usatoday.com
USA TODAY
Life
SECTION D

September 9, 2008

From the Pages of USA TODAY

# Continuous monitoring devices help adults control diabetes

New research shows that adults with type 1 diabetes who use continuous glucose monitoring devices to help manage their disease control their blood sugar better.

A clinical trial paid for by the Juvenile Diabetes Research Foundation involved 322 patients with type 1 diabetes, ages 8 to 72. They were at 10 sites coordinated by the Jaeb Center for Health Research in Tampa, Florida.

Some patients were assigned to a small continuous glucose monitoring device. The device can be attached to the body using a tiny catheter [tube] that measures blood glucose levels and produces readings every few minutes. Others were assigned to a control group using standard blood sugar monitoring. This involved manually pricking a finger for blood and testing glucose levels using a separate meter. Researchers tracked the patients for 26 weeks. Patients were analyzed by three age groups: 8 to 14 years, 15 to 24 years, and 25 years or older.

Improvements in blood sugar control were best in the continuous glucose monitoring patient group that was 25 and up. In the other age groups, patients using continuous glucose monitoring fared no better than patients using the traditional method of pricking a finger.

Though the study showed little effect of continuous glucose monitoring in children, in adults the results indicate that it can control blood sugar.

David Marrero, an endocrinologist at the Indiana University School of Medicine, says the advantage of continuous glucose monitoring is that patients can see trends that result from behavioral choices, such as food choices and when they eat, in a dynamic way.

—*Mary Brophy Marcus*

## MEASURING BLOOD SAMPLES

To measure glucose levels, you put a drop of blood on a test strip. This chemically treated strip inserts into a blood sugar meter. The meter quickly measures and displays glucose levels from the blood sample. Blood sugar meters contain small computers that process and store information. Depending upon the amount of memory in the meter, it may store results for several weeks. Some meters allow you to download data onto your personal computer and track blood sugar trends over time.

A range of lightweight, palm-sized meters is available in different sizes and colors. Special versions offer larger screens for easy viewing and talking meters for those who have a visual impairment.

## KEEPING A LOG

Doctors encourage patients to record their test results in a log, or a diary. Tracking the numbers with behaviors lets you see how various foods, activities, medications, illness, and other situations affect your blood sugar. The American Diabetes Association sells a color-coded desk diabetes management planner that highlights daily food intake, testing results, medication, and exercise. A log helps you and your diabetes care team evaluate a new treatment routine or change in medication. As one man with diabetes said, "No news is not good news as a diabetic. The more we know about our condition, the better our condition."

# CHAPTER FIVE

# MEDICATIONS AND INSULIN

Emily, aged twenty-four, was sixteen when she found out she had type 1 diabetes. "My parents both have first cousins with type 1 diabetes. So does my brother," she says. "Before I was diagnosed, our family gave blood as part of a diabetes study. Test results found evidence of an antibody that indicated I had a good chance of developing diabetes. Two years after the test, I received the diagnosis."

Because her pancreas was producing almost no insulin, Emily started taking insulin right away. "I had to be careful about what I was eating because I didn't know how to measure my blood sugar," she recalls. "Figuring out the right amount of insulin to take is a balancing act, a lot of trial and error. So the first weekend, I worked with the doctors a lot."[16]

Over time, Emily became very good at measuring her blood sugar levels every day. Now she understands how to change her insulin dosage based on what she eats and on her daily activities. She uses both long-acting and rapid-acting forms of the hormone-based medication to manage her diabetes.

Steve's weight climbed as he aged. By his sixty-first birthday, he was about 30 pounds (14 kg) overweight. His doctor told him he had type 2 diabetes, possibly triggered by gaining so much weight. Steve's blood glucose levels were not excessively high. Under doctors orders, Steve worked out, cut the number of calories he ate, and lost 10 pounds (5 kg). The weight loss helped control his blood sugar levels for a while. But after a year, they started to climb again. Eventually, Steve needed oral medication to help keep his glucose levels in a healthy range.

## THE NEXT LEVEL OF TREATMENT

Many people with type 2 diabetes can control their glucose levels through diet, weight loss, exercise, and blood sugar monitoring. Others must take medication or inject insulin to keep their glucose levels stable. People with type 1 diabetes need insulin in their treatment plan to lead a normal life.

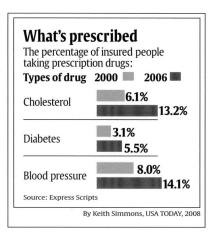

**What's prescribed**

The percentage of insured people taking prescription drugs:

| Types of drug | 2000 | 2006 |
|---|---|---|
| Cholesterol | 6.1% | 13.2% |
| Diabetes | 3.1% | 5.5% |
| Blood pressure | 8.0% | 14.1% |

Source: Express Scripts

By Keith Simmons, USA TODAY, 2008

Medications are not miracle cures. Often patients and doctors must balance a drug's benefits with its side effects. Some medications work better when taken in combination with other drugs. Even with medications, diet and exercise still play key roles in staying healthy and helping obtain better results from the insulin.

## TYPE 2 DIABETES DRUGS

Sometimes, diet and exercise fail to stabilize glucose levels in people with type 2 diabetes. The next step is for doctors to add medication to the treatment plan. The type of drug and how often it is taken depend on different factors. Doctors ask: How much do blood sugar levels need to be lowered? What age is the patient? When did diabetes first occur? What other medications is the person taking? Can the patient handle possible side effects from a specific medicine?

Several classes of drugs work to stabilize blood sugar levels. Each type of medication performs a different function inside the body. Sulfonylureas stimulate the pancreas to manufacture and release more insulin. In turn, the extra insulin lowers blood glucose levels. People who benefit from this type of drug are normal weight, take

**February 18, 2010**

From the Pages of USA TODAY

# Technology 'changing the face of health care'

A boom in medical technology over the past decade or two has led to a surge in certain medical tests and increased prescription drug use, say authors of a report that provides a snapshot of Americans'

health today. Anti-diabetic drug use by people 45 and up increased about 55% when comparing 1988–1994 with 2003–2006 figures.

*—Mary Brophy Marcus*

small amounts of insulin or none, and have had diabetes for less than five years. Possible side effects include low blood sugar, nausea, skin rash, weight gain, dizziness, and headache.

Another category of drugs inhibits or slows production and release of glucose stored in the liver. Pills called biguanides improve the way the body makes cells more sensitive to insulin. But some patients report side effects of nausea, diarrhea, swelling, weight gain, and increase of fats in the blood. These medications raise the risk of liver or kidney damage. So people taking them must be checked regularly for signs of liver or kidney disease.

The last major category of drugs blocks the stomach from giving off hormones that break down sugar. Alpha-glucosidase inhibitors slow digestion and the body's ability to absorb sugar. Doctors recommend these drugs to people who experience elevated blood sugars after eating.

Physicians often prescribe additional drugs to counteract the side effects from diabetes and diabetes drugs. Someone with diabetes

December 10, 2008

From the Pages of USA TODAY

# Diabetes drugs double women's fracture risk

L ong-term use of a popular class of oral diabetes drugs doubles the risk of bone fractures in women with type 2 diabetes, a study reports.

Researchers at Wake Forest University School of Medicine [in North Carolina] reviewed 10 previous drug trials. They found that for every 20 women in their 70s with type 2 diabetes who took thiazolidinediones (brand-names Avandia and Actos) for at least one year, one of them has a chance of suffering a fracture. In women in their mid-50s, the figure equals one fracture in every 55 women. That's more than double the normal risk for those age groups.

Avandia has been shown to increase the risk of heart attacks as well.

*—Mary Brophy Marcus*

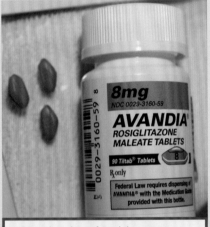

Researchers have found that some diabetes drugs, such as Avandia, can make women taking the medication more susceptible to fractures.

might also take drugs to prevent heart, kidney, and other diseases that increase with diabetes. These drugs can cause their own problems and need constant monitoring by a doctor.

Researchers constantly test new and improved diabetes medications. In the early twenty-first century, two promising drugs came on the market. They are exenatide (Byetta) and sitagliptin phosphate (Januvia). These two drugs belong to a class of drugs known as incretin mimetics. Both stimulate insulin production while curbing the liver's release of sugar. A bonus from these drugs is that they help some people lose weight. Most medications for type 2 diabetes generally cause weight gain. Added pounds are exactly what people with diabetes try to avoid. Patients who take these new drugs find they can maintain or lose weight while improving their blood sugar levels.

"I used to have a love affair with my refrigerator," said a man with diabetes after six months on Byetta. "Now I eat about half of what I used to eat. My numbers are good even for a nondiabetic now."

## TAKING INSULIN

People with type 1 diabetes need insulin to balance what their pancreas cannot use or produce. In addition, about 30 percent of people with type 2 diabetes require insulin. For these patients, oral medications alone do not keep glucose levels steady. Sometimes their medicine pushes the pancreas into overdrive to produce enough insulin. As the pancreas works harder, its ability to manufacture insulin slows or stops completely, requiring injected insulin.

In the past, scientists made insulin from cow or pig pancreases. But animal insulin sometimes caused uneven absorption and allergic reactions. Given these problems, scientists developed an artificial insulin with a chemical makeup identical to human insulin. Most people who need insulin today use the artificial form.

So far, the only ways individuals with diabetes take insulin are by injection with a tiny needle and via an insulin pump. One manufacturer used to offer insulin inhaled into the lungs. But the company stopped making the product due to increased risk of lung cancer in smokers. Insulin pills cannot work effectively to control glucose levels. Swallowing them triggers the process of digestion.

A teenager with diabetes shows the insulin pump that she uses. Since she is a long-distance runner, the pump helps keep her blood sugar stable as she exercises.

Stomach acids released during digestion break up and destroy insulin before it enters the bloodstream. Injections and pumps deliver insulin into the bloodstream. Without passing through the stomach, they can provide fuel directly to cells.

## TYPES OF INSULIN

Doctors may prescribe one or more of several types of insulin. Each works at a different rate. Rapid, or fast-acting, insulin begins working within fifteen minutes. People take this form just before eating. If they inject fast-acting insulin and delay eating, blood sugar drops to dangerous levels. So eating immediately is essential with this form of insulin.

Short-acting, or regular, insulin begins working thirty minutes after injection. This is the time the body needs to digest a meal. Short-acting insulin helps when someone isn't sure when or what they are eating.

# HONEYMOON PHASE

Shortly after beginning to take insulin, many people with type 1 diabetes experience sudden improvement. Blood sugar levels become stable, requiring less insulin to maintain good control. The improvement may last weeks, months, or a year. Some people imagine their diabetes is almost gone. Doctors call this the honeymoon phase. But just as a honeymoon ends and real married life begins, blood sugar problems return. Diabetes is a chronic illness that never goes away completely.

What causes this honeymoon phase? At the start of insulin treatment, the body may still be producing small amounts of insulin. Adding insulin by injection allows the pancreas beta cells to regain enough strength to meet the body's demand. Over time, however, the immune system continues to attack and destroy existing beta cells. Insulin production drops, and more insulin injections are needed to make up for the loss.

Intermediate- and long-acting insulins last longer in the system. Each contains chemicals that slow how they behave. As a result, fewer injections are needed throughout the day. Still, people using these forms must follow a regimented meal plan of eating measured amounts of food at certain times during the day.

Rapid-acting insulin requires more injections but allows for greater flexibility in eating choices and activity. Most people who require insulin take a long-acting insulin once or twice a day. They use rapid-acting insulin before eating and to correct high blood sugar. Combinations of short- and intermediate-acting insulin come premixed. A combination of drugs offers the option of less planning ahead, something people with diabetes appreciate.

The types and amounts of insulin people take depend on many factors: body size, how sensitive cells are to small amounts of insulin produced by the pancreas, activity level, and food selections for snacks and meals. Requirements vary from one person to another. Some people experience better results from short-acting insulin taken in smaller doses several times a day. Others respond better to long-acting insulin. Many people with diabetes take both types.

Most people who need insulin test their blood sugar six to eight times a day to determine how much insulin to inject before or after eating. "Once you know the amount of glucose, you can figure out how much insulin to take," Jared explains. "I test on average four times a day. A lot of times I know what a particular extreme, either high or low blood sugar, will feel like. I test my blood sugar, and if it confirms my thinking, I know how much insulin to inject."

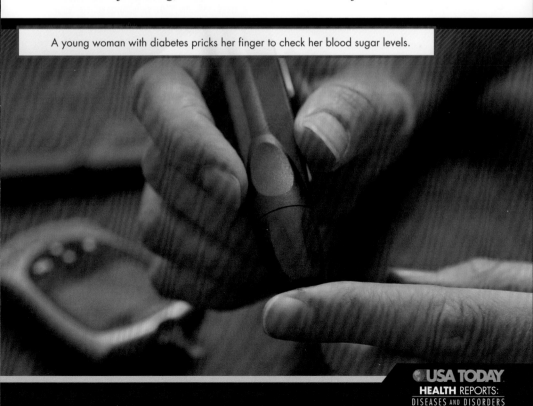

A young woman with diabetes pricks her finger to check her blood sugar levels.

Even with careful planning, insulin programs need adjusting over time. The disease may improve or worsen, other health factors may develop, or new forms of insulin and medication may become available. Researchers continue to look for ways to make insulin more effective and easier to administer.

### INJECTING INSULIN

To inject insulin, people with diabetes use a syringe with a needle attached, an insulin pen, or a jet injector. The most common method of insulin delivery is by syringe, especially if you mix two types of insulin.

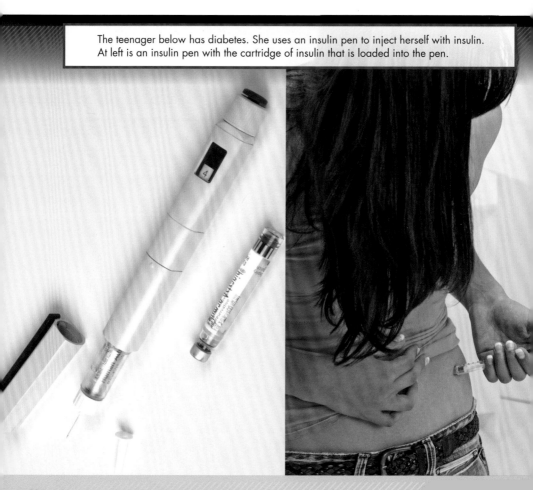

The teenager below has diabetes. She uses an insulin pen to inject herself with insulin. At left is an insulin pen with the cartridge of insulin that is loaded into the pen.

A pen injector looks like a fat marker. Users select the correct dose on a dial before injecting the insulin. Pens store easily and require fewer supplies. Jet injectors shoot insulin through the skin with high-pressure air rather than a needle. This method is expensive and can be painful.

Insulin works best when injected into fatty tissue under the skin. From there, the insulin goes directly into the bloodstream. The abdomen offers the most effective place to distribute insulin evenly. But many people find it easier to inject insulin into their hips, thighs, or upper arms.

Another delivery method is the insulin pump. The pump looks like a pager-sized electronic device. Users wear the pump outside the body on a belt or inside a pocket. Pumps deliver a small, steady flow of insulin throughout the day. Each pump can be programmed to deliver varying amounts of glucose into the system. Insulin goes through a flexible plastic tube inserted under the skin, usually in the abdomen. Programming ensures better blood sugar control by allowing users to customize their insulin delivery based on changes, such as with physical activity, meals, and illness.

Newer models of pumps combine insulin delivery with a glucose meter. Parents of children with diabetes often prefer using a pump because they can give insulin without repeated injections. Pumps allow for a more normal lifestyle. But they cost more than pens, need additional supplies, and may require more attention.

"Pumps are best for people who take the time to constantly monitor their blood sugar," said Melissa, a social worker who's had diabetes since the age of twelve. "It forces you to test more, which is probably why people who prefer pumps have better control. You can give yourself smaller amounts of insulin, like quarters and eighths. But you feel constantly burdened. The pump is what kids start with when it's up to parents to test."

# CHAPTER SIX

# UNCONTROLLED DIABETES

A bby, at the age of eighteen, preferred not to think about having type 1 diabetes. She rarely tested her blood sugar in front of anyone. She told only her closest friends she had diabetes. Abby took insulin and tested her blood sugar at bedtime. But she refused to do everything she could to keep her diabetes under control.

For Abby, having diabetes wasn't cool—but being thin was. She received positive attention for losing weight. But her weight loss was not a good sign. It meant that her sugar levels were unstable. She constantly drank liquids because too much water left her body. Her lips and tongue always seemed dry. She often felt tired and out of sorts. Although friends thought Abby looked great, she was getting sicker.

One day after basketball practice, Abby stood still. She seemed confused. Her speech sounded slurred. Since she never mentioned her diabetes, neither her teammates nor the coach knew what was wrong. Then Abby fainted. The coach recognized that Abby was in serious trouble and called an ambulance. The paramedics determined that Abby's blood sugar was dangerously low. They revived her with a shot of glucagon. The hormone prompted her liver to convert glycogen into glucose and release it into the bloodstream quickly. At the hospital, doctors admitted Abby. They wanted hospital staff to help her plan how to better control her diabetes.

Dangerous problems can occur even when diabetes treatment generally works. Illness or a change in diet or activity can throw blood sugar levels off balance. Unstable glucose levels can trigger hypoglycemia or hyperglycemia. Sugar levels that are too high or too low eventually destroy cells throughout the body, causing a range of complications. In addition, uncontrolled glucose levels release toxic acids into the blood and urine. This causes a serious condition known as ketoacidosis. But any of these extreme situations signals that the body is in trouble and requires immediate attention.

## HYPOGLYCEMIA: LOW BLOOD SUGAR

Hypoglycemia results when blood sugar levels plunge too low. Excessively low glucose levels may prompt uncontrolled sweating and feeling jittery, drained, confused, or extremely hungry. As glucose levels drop lower, hearing problems, blurred vision, and

## FACTORS THAT AFFECT BLOOD SUGAR LEVELS

Anything that puts stress on the body can affect blood sugar regulation and the body's use of glucose. Glucose levels may change in response to many factors, including:

• food amounts, choices, and times of meals and snacks

• exercise

• alcoholic beverages

• hormone changes

• illness

• stress

• medications

• lack of sleep

headache may occur. If left untreated, low blood sugar can cause loss of consciousness or coma.

Other names for hypoglycemia are insulin reaction or insulin shock. These names reflect the sudden drop in blood sugar levels from an overload of insulin in the system. Hypoglycemia may result from injecting too much insulin, eating too little food, being sick, exercising, or drinking alcohol. Rapidly falling sugar levels are dangerous because the nervous system relies on glucose to work correctly. Without proper glucose levels, all systems suffer.

"Low blood sugars. Those are the worst," Jared says. "I like to think of it as [dropping] a notch on the evolutionary totem pole. Your brain doesn't work. Sometimes you can't even help yourself. All of a sudden it takes effort just to reach for a Coke."

Hypoglycemia can be treated easily by eating or drinking something that contains sugar, such as fruit juice or an orange. Problems from occasional low blood sugar usually cause no permanent damage. Still, diabetes educators suggest that people with diabetes always carry snacks with them in case of emergency. Snacks that provide quick energy include hard candies, fruit juice, skim milk, raisins, or sugar cubes. Chewable glucose tablets sold at drugstores also give the body a rush of sugar and are easy to carry.

Drinking orange juice is a way to get your blood sugar back up.

## EMERGENCY IDENTIFICATION

High or low blood sugars increase the risk of a serious medical emergency. Problems can develop quickly and among strangers. In some instances, a person having a diabetic reaction may look weird, drunk, or scary. To alert others about what is happening, people with diabetes wear a medical identification bracelet or necklace. These tell strangers that the wearer has diabetes and needs immediate medical attention.

The identifying jewelry provides emergency numbers to contact. Paramedics are trained to check the wrist and the neck for this lifesaving jewelry. "I wear a medical alert bracelet, and many people ask about it," Emily says. "I think it's important that people I spend a lot of time with know in case something happens."

## HYPERGLYCEMIA: HIGH BLOOD SUGAR

*Hyperglycemia* is another word for high blood sugar levels. Signs of hyperglycemia include extreme thirst, frequent urination, blurred vision, vomiting, and unexplained weight loss. Left untreated, hyperglycemia can lead to weakness, confusion, and cool hands and feet. Another danger sign is dehydration, when too much water leaves the body, causing dry mouth and thirst. Over time, hyperglycemia damages small and large blood vessels. Illness, hormone changes, and stress can trigger hyperglycemia. So can drinking alcoholic beverages, eating too much, and inactivity.

# KETOACIDOSIS: INCREASED BLOOD ACIDS

When Jared first learned he had diabetes, he hardly realized anything was wrong. Gradually, he learned the warning signs, including frequent bathroom trips, thirst, and a different taste in his mouth. "Your saliva has different compounds that taste sour," Jared notes. "You can feel your salivary glands produce this sour taste."

The compounds Jared noticed are called ketones. These are toxic fatty acids that are produced when the body breaks down fat. When too little insulin is available to allow cells to receive glucose, the body turns to fat for fuel. As a result, ketones are released into the bloodstream and urine. Increased acids produce the bitterness that Jared tastes when his sugar levels rise. This condition is called diabetic ketoacidosis (DKA).

DKA usually occurs when diabetes is undiagnosed, untreated, or uncontrolled. Illness, stress, or missing an insulin shot can stimulate acid buildup as well. DKA is more common among people with type 1 diabetes, but it can happen with type 2. Some warning signs are the same as for diabetes: dry mouth and frequent urination. Other signs appear more flulike, including:

- stomach pain
- nausea or flushed skin
- sour, fruity breath
- fever or flushed skin
- rapid breathing
- loss of appetite
- weakness
- sleepiness

If you experience these symptoms, test your blood sugar level for ketones, since excess acid spills into urine. Doctors recommend testing with chemically treated strips that change color when dipped into urine. The strips show whether ketone levels are low, medium, or high by the color they turn. A more accurate way to test at home is to buy a meter that signals results.

DKA requires immediate medical attention. Insulin injections usually bring sugar and ketone levels back to normal. But you may also need to drink large amounts of fluids to replace lost liquid and nutrients. Without immediate care, DKA can lead to loss of consciousness and death. With prompt treatment, however, symptoms usually disappear completely.

## HEART AND BLOOD VESSEL DISEASE

Cardiovascular disease—heart and blood vessel problems—is the major cause of death among people with diabetes. According to *USA Today* reporter Mary Brophy Marcus, "More than 65 percent of people with diabetes die from heart disease or stroke (when a blood vessel to the brain bursts or is blocked). And diabetes can cause heart attacks earlier in life."

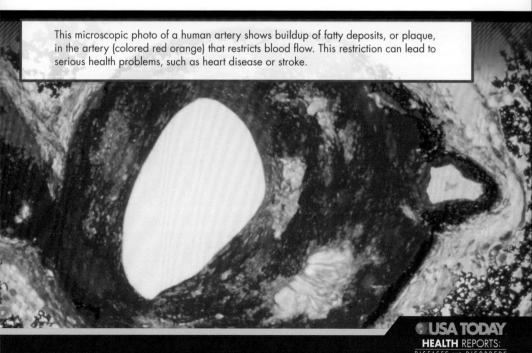

This microscopic photo of a human artery shows buildup of fatty deposits, or plaque, in the artery (colored red orange) that restricts blood flow. This restriction can lead to serious health problems, such as heart disease or stroke.

www.usatoday.com

**USA TODAY**

**Life**

SECTION D

June 8, 2009

From the Pages of USA TODAY

# Diabetics with heart disease: Meds vs. surgery

Prompt bypass [heart] surgery holds no advantage over intensive drug therapy in many patients with type 2 diabetes when it comes to dying from strokes or heart attacks, new research suggests.

Results from a study that explored the best treatment for patients with both type 2 diabetes and stable coronary heart disease were reported Sunday at the American Diabetes Association's 69th scientific conference in New Orleans [Louisiana]. The study, a multicenter trial led by the University of Pittsburgh [Pennsylvania] Graduate School of Public Health, took place at 49 medical centers in six countries over five years.

The study evaluated two surgery approaches as well as a drug-focused approach in 2,368 people with type 2 diabetes and stable coronary artery disease to help determine the best way to reduce deaths and cardiovascular events (heart attacks and stroke).

Intensive medical, or drug-based, treatment combined with either prompt bypass surgery or angioplasty (balloons through the arteries) was compared with intensive medical treatment alone.

Survival rates were 88% overall, says Montefiore Medical Center [in New York] investigator Joel Zonszein.

"A 12% mortality [death] rate at five years in this population is wonderful. It shows they do very well when treated well with medication." Cardiovascular-related mortality rates for diabetics are typically in the range of about 22% to 28%, he says.

"The study reinforces that for people with diabetes and mild heart disease, medical therapy works, and works very well," Zonszein says,

[Following] a medication plan is key to heart health, says Richard Kahn, chief scientific and medical officer of the ADA. "Faithfully taking meds and keeping blood glucose under control works and is certainly less expensive, less intrusive and less painful than surgical intervention."

—*Mary Brophy Marcus*

Diabetes interferes with how blood circulates through the body. Sugar buildup in the blood thickens and slows its flow through small and large blood vessels. Reduced blood flow causes less glucose, oxygen, and other nutrients to reach cells in the brain and heart. Without these substances, cells become injured or die.

Cell death from elevated blood sugar damages arteries, the large vessels that carry blood from the heart to body tissues and organs. The damage allows fatty deposits, or plaque, to form in the arteries, This process clogs or narrows them. Too much fat in the bloodstream drives up blood pressure, the force of blood against artery walls. High blood pressure contributes to heart disease. People with diabetes are two to four times more likely than people without the illness to develop heart disease. Their risk of stroke increases fivefold.

## NERVE DAMAGE

The nervous system contains a large network of nerves that carry messages between the brain and other body parts. High levels of glucose can damage nerves anywhere along the network. When damage occurs, messages may slow, send the wrong signal, or stop transmitting altogether.

Nerve damage, called neuropathy, contributes to a wide range of problems, depending on which nerves are affected. For example, decreased communication to body organs can disturb digestion, breathing, bladder and bowel function, and sexual performance. You may experience pain, numbness, and tingling in feet, arms, and hands, and loss of balance.

Someone who does not feel pain might not notice a cut or a wound. Without feeling, these areas become more prone to bruising and infection. As infection spreads, cells in the limb can die. In some cases, doctors find they must surgically remove the infected limb

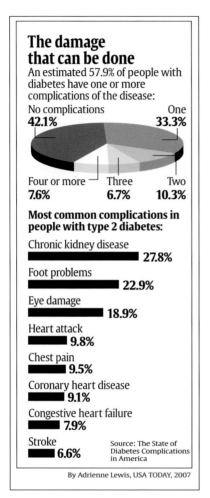

## The damage that can be done

An estimated 57.9% of people with diabetes have one or more complications of the disease:

No complications
**42.1%**

One
**33.3%**

Four or more
**7.6%**

Three
**6.7%**

Two
**10.3%**

**Most common complications in people with type 2 diabetes:**

Chronic kidney disease
**27.8%**

Foot problems
**22.9%**

Eye damage
**18.9%**

Heart attack
**9.8%**

Chest pain
**9.5%**

Coronary heart disease
**9.1%**

Congestive heart failure
**7.9%**

Stroke
**6.6%**

Source: The State of Diabetes Complications in America

By Adrienne Lewis, USA TODAY, 2007

due to serious infection. About 65 percent of people with diabetes experience some form of damage to their nervous system.

## EYE DAMAGE

Tiny blood vessels nourish the back of the eye, called the retina. The retina senses light to produce images. High blood sugar damages eye blood vessels, interfering with incoming light and making vision blurry. Problems in the retina are referred to as retinopathy.

Eye damage worsens the longer diabetes remains untreated or unstable. As blood thickens from diabetes, vessels in the retina swell or bulge. Weakened, swollen blood vessels can leak blood into the eye, reducing vision more. In some cases, new blood vessels form as scar tissue. These vessels are weak and spread wildly, further interfering with vision.

Blood vessel changes eventually affect almost all people with type 1 diabetes and more than six in ten with type 2. Poorly controlled diabetes remains the leading cause of blindness in U.S. adults between the ages of 20 and 74. People with diabetes can lower their risk of diabetes-related eye problems by keeping glucose levels within a normal range and having yearly eye exams. Eye doctors can detect

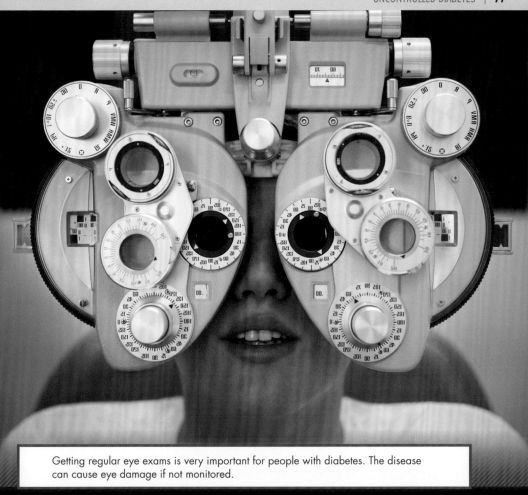

Getting regular eye exams is very important for people with diabetes. The disease can cause eye damage if not monitored.

signs of eye disease before patients notice symptoms. Treatment usually stops eye damage from progressing if caught early.

## KIDNEY DISEASE

Diabetes interferes with the kidneys' normal filtering system. Your two kidneys sit in back of your abdomen on both sides of the spine and just below the waist. Their job is to receive oxygen-rich blood from the heart, remove waste products from the blood, and discharge waste in urine.

Kidney disease, or nephropathy, can develop when blood sugar levels remain elevated over a period of time. Studies indicate that kidney changes occur within three years of high glucose levels. Sugar damages the tiny blood vessels that strain waste from the blood. When waste products remain in the system, they crowd out nutrients and cause other problems.

Symptoms of kidney damage include swollen feet, ankles, and hands and fatigue. If untreated, kidney disease can lead to difficulty concentrating, nausea and vomiting, loss of appetite, high blood pressure, and eventually kidney failure. Total kidney failure takes time to develop. But severe damage often happens without warning, which makes the problem more dangerous. According to the American Diabetes Association, "Kidneys have so much extra filtering ability that noticeable problems will not appear until 80 percent of the kidneys are damaged."

Urine tests can pick up early signs of kidney disease. Therefore, if you have diabetes, regular exams are important. But you can lessen the risk of kidney problems overall by lowering high blood pressure. This reduces stress on the kidneys' delicate blood vessels. Maintaining a healthy weight and reducing the amount of salt, or sodium, in your diet helps lower blood pressure.

The longer someone has diabetes, the greater the threat of kidney disease. Three in ten people with type 1 and one in ten with type 2 diabetes eventually experience some form of kidney disease. Diabetes is the main cause of kidney failure in the United States.

## MEMORY LOSS

Recent studies link diabetes with dementia and Alzheimer's disease. Both conditions damage the brain and cause memory loss. According

**April 15, 2009**

From the Pages of USA TODAY

# Type 2 diabetics more susceptible to dementia

People with diabetes who have low-blood-sugar episodes serious enough to land them in the hospital have a higher risk of being diagnosed with dementia later in life, new research suggests.

Researchers evaluated the health records of more than 16,000 people with type 2 diabetes, tracking episodes of severe hypoglycemia—low blood sugar—over 22 years. They then followed patients for four more years to track diagnoses of dementia.

Compared with patients with no hypoglycemia, patients with one severe hypoglycemic episode had 26% increased risk of dementia; those with two episodes had an 80% increased risk; and people who had had three or more episodes had nearly double the risk, the authors reported in today's *Journal of the American Medical Association.*

—*Mary Brophy Marcus*

to these studies, people with type 2 diabetes are twice as likely to develop Alzheimer's disease as people without diabetes. Scientists believe that circulation problems caused by diabetes interfere with blood flow to the brain. Reduced blood flow results in damaged brain cells that influence memory.

Researchers are investigating a destructive protein called amyloid, which is involved in both Alzheimer's disease and diabetes. When amyloid clumps together, it forms gooey plaques in the brain. These masses cause the memory problems found in Alzheimer's disease. In people with type 2 diabetes, amyloid builds up in the pancreas. But too much insulin in the brain—caused when cells resist insulin—can lead to amyloid buildup in the brain.

# INFECTIONS

People with uncontrolled diabetes experience more infections than the average person. High blood sugar levels hamper the immune system's ability to destroy germs that attack the body. Once germs enter the body, they feed on extra sugar in the blood and spread disease. Elevated blood sugar levels may destroy the very nerves that provide a warning system for problems. People with diabetes face a greater risk of infection in the skin, feet, gums, and vagina. Without treatment, infections can lead to more serious problems.

Diabetes educators also advise patients to brush and floss regularly to reduce the threat of gum disease. They counsel patients to check their feet daily for cuts or other wounds and to stay alert to the most minor injury.

New research indicates that temperature may help people without feeling in their feet detect possible infections. A rise in body temperature generally signals infection. One doctor found that the same is true for the bottom of feet. He encourages his patients with diabetes to keep track of the temperature of their feet using a special infrared thermometer that senses heat. If either foot varies in temperature, the patient should stay off the warmer foot and see a doctor. The doctor believes that this simple technique prevents sores and more serious problems from developing.

> Handheld infrared thermometers like this one can help people with diabetes detect foot problems at home.

## PREVENTING PROBLEMS

Learning about everything that can go wrong if you have diabetes can be scary. But a diagnosis of diabetes does not automatically mean that you'll encounter complications. Many factors play a role in how the disease develops. Anyone with diabetes can take steps to manage the disease and help prevent complications:

- Keep tight control of glucose levels, and follow your treatment plan.
- Schedule a yearly physical exam and appointments with the eye doctor, foot doctor, and dentist.
- See your diabetes doctor for regular checkups.
- Brush and floss your teeth twice a day.
- Stay up to date with vaccinations for flu and other illnesses.
- Take good care of your feet.
- Don't smoke.
- Avoid alcohol.
- Find healthy ways to relieve stress. (Check out the tips in the next chapter.)

# CHAPTER SEVEN

# LIFE WITH DIABETES

*Brianna, twenty years old, discovered she had type 1 diabetes when she was fifteen. Her older sister had been diagnosed at the age of twelve, so the family recognized the symptoms. After Brianna was diagnosed, she attended classes at a local hospital to learn how to inject insulin and balance her food intake. Within a few weeks, following a diabetes treatment plan came naturally to her. She found it fairly easy to control her glucose levels. Most of the time, she didn't think about her disease. But after her last doctor's appointment, Brianna realized that she didn't want to have diabetes anymore. Maybe it was the constant checking of blood sugar—in the morning, after meals, and at bedtime. The routine was getting annoying and old. Every time she went to the doctor, her care team discussed changes she needed to improve her health. This was probably true for everybody. But knowing that her diabetes would last forever hit her hard.*

## A LIFELONG ILLNESS

Medical professionals cannot offer a quick fix or cure for diabetes. People with the condition must pay attention to their diet, activities, and other health issues all day, every day, their whole life. Losing weight, adjusting diet and medication, and monitoring glucose levels take time and energy. Even under the best circumstances, managing diabetes can be difficult. But many people have found ways to make life with diabetes easier.

Understanding the ups and downs of having diabetes can be helpful. Everyone normally goes through periods of feeling sad, happy, or angry. A long-term disease adds extra challenges and increases the likelihood these feelings will occur. The diabetes care team can help with understanding these reactions and offer tips for getting through tough periods. They have information about joining a support group, where people with diabetes share their emotional journey and offer suggestions for making life with a long-term illness easier. Others in the same situation have figured out ways to relieve the stresses of diabetes.

## MIXED FEELINGS

Upon first learning you have diabetes, you may feel overwhelmed, afraid, worried, sad, or angry. These are all common reactions. Over time, your feelings may seesaw. Unexpected problems may spark disappointment or embarrassment about having a body that refuses to work properly.

One in five people with diabetes experiences depression—a deep sadness or sense of hopelessness that continues for weeks or months. People who are depressed no longer find joy in everyday activities. They may lack energy to care for their diabetes. If you or someone you know expresses sadness that lasts more than two weeks for no apparent reason, seek professional help. Counseling or psychotherapy, support groups, medication, or a combination of these treatments can help ease depression.

Feeling depressed after a diabetes diagnosis is common.

Everyone with diabetes handles challenges differently. Some people deny they have the disease. They keep it a secret from friends, teachers, and coworkers. Other people talk openly about the condition and feel comfortable testing their blood sugar and injecting insulin in public.

"Diabetes is an invasion of the body and sense of self," says Melissa. "I think it's made me look toward the future more than I would otherwise. Diabetes can also make you worry a lot. I might obsess about having diabetes but not do enough. Other people get very compulsive, testing and watching everything they eat and do."

A few people focus on their disease to an unhealthy extreme. They dwell on diabetes to the point that it interferes with relationships, leisure activities, and a balanced lifestyle. They use their condition as a crutch for failures or faults. Either avoiding or fixating on diabetes can be unhealthy if it lasts longer than a phase. These feelings can be dealt with by talking with a professional. With time, however, most people learn to accept and live with their diabetes.

## CHILDREN WITH DIABETES

Diabetes is a family affair, especially when children have the disease. Life changes for everyone in the household. A diabetes treatment plan may require particular snacks, mealtimes, and planned activities. Creating a balance between diabetes planning and everyday activities helps ease the stress that diabetes can place on families.

## DIABETES CAMP

Children with diabetes can attend camps just for kids like them. Diabetes camps tailor meals to individual food plans and hire on-staff medical teams with diabetes experience. At these special camps,

www.usatoday.com

USA TODAY
**Life**
SECTION D

**January 11, 2010**

From the Pages of USA TODAY

# Type 1 affects every aspect of daily life

Type 1 diabetes is not one of those medical conditions for which you can just pop a pill and then forget about it.

It forces you to think about every bite you put into your mouth, every activity you do, says Andrew Drexler, director of the Gonda Diabetes Center at UCLA [University of California at Los Angeles]. "It's always there. You can never get away from it."

Type 1 is usually diagnosed in children and young adults. The most serious short-term problem is hypoglycemia, or low blood sugar, which can cause wooziness and disorientation. If it strikes while someone's driving, for instance, that person is at risk for an accident. If blood sugar dips severely low, coma and death can occur.

A diagnosis can have a significant effect on mental health, says Duke [University in North Carolina] endocrinologist Susan Spratt. "Patients go through the stage of grief," Spratt says. "They mourn the life they had before diabetes, a life when they could eat, exercise and sleep spontaneously."

The key to managing the disease: Check blood sugar often and use insulin and other medicines to keep blood sugars steady, Drexler says.

And Drexler says patients should remain positive. "We have to give our patients hope that the medical community is working on a cure. Type 1 diabetes is treatable. You can live a full life and grow up, have a family and be anything you want to be."

*—Mary Brophy Marcus*

kids of all ages can have fun while getting to know other children with diabetes. Camps are located throughout the United States. Families can locate a camp at www.childrenwithdiabetes.com/ camps or through the American Diabetes Association.

Parents of young children with diabetes have two extra jobs. They must manage the disease and help their child cope with it. A

Attending a diabetes camp, such as this one in Ontario, Canada, can help children meet other children with diabetes.

parent's tasks include staying alert to symptoms, monitoring blood sugar, injecting insulin, and preparing foods as planned. Diabetes requires parents to plan ahead for situations, such as birthday parties, sleepovers, camp, trick-or-treating, and any other potential trouble spots. Many parents devise creative ways to help their child enjoy and fit into everyday situations. Parents may prepare healthy snacks to send with their child to a party or a sleepover. That way, their child has something to eat with the other children. Or they might host a Halloween party at home. At home they can control the treats and give presents instead of candy to trick-or-treaters.

Diabetes in the family can overwhelm everyone at times. Parents often blame themselves for their child's condition. They worry that they fed their child the wrong foods or passed on a family disease. Brothers and sisters may feel that the child with diabetes gets special attention for being sick. Families need to strike a balance between managing the disease and addressing each family member's needs.

"In a way, it was like having an infant again," remembers Jared's mother, Ann. "The condition was a lot to get used to."

**USA TODAY Snapshots®**

**Sugar-free celebrations**

Percentage of public elementary students whose schools restrict sweets during class parties:

No restrictions **48%**

School policy restricts sweets **37%**

Some classes allow **15%**

Source: Bridging the Gap, Health Policy Center, Institute for Health Research and Policy, University of Illinois at Chicago, 2010

By Michelle Healy and Alejandro Gonzalez, USA TODAY, 2010

## DIABETES AND SCHOOL

Going to school presents special challenges for children with diabetes. They need to eat more frequently to keep blood sugar levels stable. They may be unable to eat the same foods as their classmates at lunchtime or for snacks. Children with diabetes may encounter discrimination or unfair treatment from people who know little about their disease. Classmates might tease or bully a classmate they view as different. Some teachers cannot understand why a child needs to leave the room, keep food in class, or sit on the sidelines during physical activity. Situations like these can make a child with diabetes feel different.

Parents find it helpful to work closely with teachers and principals to come up with strategies that work. Sometimes that means bending some school rules. Students with diabetes must be allowed to eat

Many families pack a special lunch for their children with diabetes. This way parents can be sure their children are eating the right foods while at school.

in class, stop exercising, or leave the classroom to visit the school nurse or test blood sugar. Teachers can help set the tone so that students respect one another's differences. They need to understand what diabetes is and how to help their students with the condition.

Children spend much of their day in school, making teachers key players in helping students with diabetes stay healthy. But parents should alert bus drivers, librarians, lunchroom attendants, and other school personnel who come in contact with their children as well.

"The school nurse and I talked every day about how Jared was doing," Ann remembers. "The nurse checked his blood sugar every day."

Some parents and children make a presentation to the class to help other students understand more about diabetes. Knowing about a condition reduces fear, teasing, and bullying. Classmates learn they cannot catch diabetes. They discover what treatment involves. Equally important, classmates and teachers learn that people with diabetes are more than their illness. Their classmates with diabetes are just like them, with the same range of abilities, interests, and hopes.

Sometimes, teachers or school administrators resist making

**Life**
SECTION D
November 2, 2009

From the Pages of USA TODAY

# More kids have diabetes, fewer schools have nurses

Christopher should have started kindergarten last year. But when his mother, Marileida, tried to enroll him in 2008, she was told Mount Hope Elementary School [in the Bronx, New York,] did not have the resources to care for Christopher, who has type 1 diabetes and was too young to recognize when his blood sugar was slipping dangerously low.

Though Marileida said she'd quit her job and come to help, the administration suggested she send her son to another school that could better serve his needs.

Christopher now attends PS [public school] 28, but it has taken lengthy negotiations with a system that doesn't speak her language and quitting her job to get [Marileida's] son into his neighborhood school, she says through a translator.

Although more schools have fewer full-time nurses while, experts say, there is an increasing number of children being diagnosed with both type 1 and type 2 diabetes, many schools are successfully adapting to the needs of these kids. Yet, many schools are still falling short.

Making inquiries, Marileida learned that though PS 28 does not have a school nurse, a medical clinic for hospital students is housed right in the PS 28 building. Spanish-speaking staff there told her they could help Christopher, who now visits the clinic as many as four times a day for blood sugar checks, insulin and snacks if needed.

Students with diabetes benefit from a team approach, says endocrinologist Frederick Schwenk. He says multiple staff members—everyone from cafeteria workers and bus drivers to gym teachers and the principal—should know about a child's medical condition and what to do in case of an emergency.

—*Mary Brophy Marcus*

accommodations for children with diabetes. Parents do have resources to encourage change. Disability laws guarantee all children the right to an education.

# TEENS WITH DIABETES

"Doctors suggest testing blood sugar before every meal," says Melissa. "They tell us to take enough insulin to control ourselves. Then we should test and take insulin again a half hour after the meal. You tell me how many teens are going to want to do this when they are out with friends or alone. Teenagers—and adults—don't always know what they're going to eat during a meal. They can't plan appropriately. I still have to force myself, and I'm an adult."

Teenage years can be complicated enough without diabetes. Hormone changes confuse the body and emotions, producing a range of feelings. If diabetes enters the mix, life becomes much more complex.

On the physical level, hormone changes can affect diabetes control and insulin resistance. On the emotional level, diabetes interferes with the normal tensions between parents and children. Teens want to be independent. They like to experiment and act spontaneously. These natural longings run counter to the tight control diabetes requires.

Parents may find letting go difficult because they worry about their teen's health. Teens with diabetes may feel deprived and frustrated. They may rebel by eating the wrong foods, not getting enough sleep, or drinking alcohol. They might refuse to test their blood sugar or take their insulin. But sooner or later, these behaviors catch up with them, which leads to health problems.

With time, however, most teens figure out how to keep themselves safe and still have fun. They reach out to friends, rather than keep their condition a secret. They learn how to deal with diabetes in social situations. For example, if blood sugar levels drop, alert teens ask someone else to drive the car. Or they sit out during part of a sports game. They remember to bring healthy snacks whenever they go out. They choose friends who will support them.

www.usatoday.com

USA TODAY

**Life**

SECTION D

**October 27, 2008**

From the Pages of USA TODAY

# Hope for diabetics

Sixteen-year-old Nick Jonas fought back tears as he performed "A Little Bit Longer," a song he wrote about his struggle with diabetes. "On the day that I got diagnosed, I heard about this event [The Carousel of Hope Ball to benefit the Barbara Davis Center for Childhood Diabetes in Denver, Colorado]. And I knew it was something that I wanted to be part of. To perform here is a dream come true for us and for me. It's truly an honor."

The diagnosis changed the family, said brother Kevin, 20. "It was hard for all of us. When it first happened, we didn't understand what diabetes was. So immediately we searched it online. Once we understood that he was going to be OK, we were way more comforted. He's doing really well with it, and there are times when we have to be there for each other, and with Nick's diabetes, there are times that you can't control it. And we just have to be there."

—*Kelley L. Carter*

Nick Jonas *(left)* wrote a song about dealing with diabetes as a teenager. He is shown here with his older brothers, Joe *(center)* and Kevin *(right)*, who with him make up the Jonas Brothers, a pop rock group.

# SUPPORTING A FRIEND WITH DIABETES

If your friend, family member, or other loved one has diabetes, here are some ways you can help them.

Do:

- Treat your friend normally.
- Ask your friend what signs point to trouble.
- Ask what you should do in case of trouble.
- Stay with a friend in trouble.
- Tell your friend something positive each day.

Don't:

- Nag.
- Tell friends with diabetes what they can and cannot do, unless you see risky behavior.
- Monitor what your friend eats or drinks.
- Tempt or pressure your friend to eat or drink anything he or she turns down.
- Blame a friend for emotional or physical highs and lows.

"I think I've always been lucky in that most of my friends are just interested in knowing about diabetes," Emily says. "I believe they look out for me. In high school, my friends made sure I ate enough at lunch. If I had low blood sugar, they walked with me to the nurse's office. In college, my friends joined my family in a fund-raising diabetes walk. My brother and I don't hide diabetes in public. But I might be a bit more careful about whipping out needles with a new date. From time to time someone is grossed out by needles, and it's understandable. In general, everyone is very supportive and helpful."

## REDUCING STRESS

"Diabetes is an inconvenience," says Carl, who has type 2 diabetes. "I take my insulin supplies everywhere and plan before I go. It looks like I'm carrying a purse around with me. Before meals at restaurants, I have to excuse myself to go to the bathroom and check my glucose level or inject insulin. I can't stay and talk with my date. When I have low blood sugar, I get light-headed. Sometimes when I delay taking insulin, I have low-grade pain throughout my body. It means sugar is stealing energy from my body cells. I have my challenges, but I'm happy to deal with them. The alternative is much worse."

Having chronic illness is stressful. Following daily insulin routines, managing blood sugar levels, and dealing with pain can take a toll on the most laid-back person. The more challenges from diabetes, the more stress it can cause. And stress affects blood sugar levels, creating a downward spiral. Hormones in the body that respond to stress alter body chemistry. They either cause blood sugar levels to spike or plunge. In turn, these stress hormones can increase insulin resistance and raise blood pressure.

## Diabetes and Smoking

Diabetes and smoking don't mix. Smoking reduces the amount of oxygen reaching body tissues and raises blood sugar levels. These factors make maintaining healthy diabetes control more difficult. Smoking and diabetes contribute to a higher risk of infection, heart disease, stroke, nerve damage, and birth defects. Cutting back on smoking helps reduce some of the negative effects. But it's best to stop smoking altogether or never start, especially if you have diabetes.

Managing and reducing stress is critical to overall health for people with diabetes. One study found that people with type 2 diabetes who included stress management techniques in their routine care significantly reduced their average blood glucose levels. But eliminating stress entirely is unrealistic. Some stress is part of everyday life for everyone. Instead, doctors counsel people with diabetes to look for ways to reduce stresses in their lives and better manage what comes their way.

"There are conditions in our life that are chronic. They're not going to go away. They just can't be fixed. The real way of managing that is to come to terms on the inside with ourselves, with our own reactions to whatever the world is giving us," says Dr. Jeffrey Brantley of Duke University Medical Center in Durham, North Carolina.

Various activities and techniques reduce stress. Exercise is one of the best because it helps control blood sugar and weight. "Exercise makes me feel better able to cope with life," says Jared. The following additional strategies help people with diabetes manage stress and stay healthy.

## PLANNING AHEAD

This sounds simple, but how many people really plan ahead? Most fly out the door two seconds before a bus is due, or they grab an apple on the way out the door in the morning. Yet preparing for situations before they happen reduces stress.

For people with diabetes, planning ahead becomes even more important. The reason is they need to know what to do in case of low or high blood sugar levels and have the correct supplies on hand. Planning ahead involves working with your care team to create a written treatment program that includes actions to follow during medical emergencies.

The American Diabetes Association recommends keeping a packed emergency kit. The kit should contain diabetes supplies for three days, including medications and insulin; quick-acting glucose tablets; snacks; injection supplies; testing materials; and batteries for meters, monitors, or pumps. The kit should also contain emergency contacts, doctor's orders, and names of school staff or coworkers who can help.

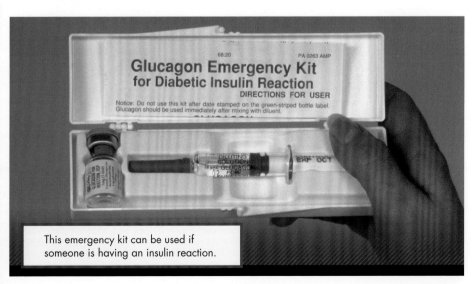

This emergency kit can be used if someone is having an insulin reaction.

Planning ahead involves preparing for situations that could interfere with following a normal diet, testing blood sugar, or taking insulin. For example, before going to a party or out for a day at the beach, consider what snacks to take; where and when to test blood sugar; and where to inject insulin privately, if this is a concern. Other situations that require planning ahead include travel, holidays, dates, long test situations, sports games, and other special events.

## SUPPORT GROUPS

Many people with diabetes and their family members find support groups helpful. Regular group meetings provide a safe place to talk about diabetes with people who understand what living with the disease is like. A support group offers a relaxed setting where members feel accepted and understood. Group members share tips and information and suggest ideas for dealing with diabetes.

Support groups are available for people of all ages. There are special groups for family members who need a place to talk about their spouse, child, or parent with diabetes. The American Diabetes Association lists where to find support groups in your area.

## RELAXATION TECHNIQUES

A variety of relaxation techniques can help relieve stress. Listening to music and deep breathing lower blood pressure and reduce stress. Anyone can arrange these activities without special training, travel, or expense.

Another easy method to reduce stress involves progressive muscle relaxation. With this activity, you sit or lie in a comfortable position. Then you focus on tightening and loosening muscles in each body part, one at a time. "It's a very simple technique in which people learn to tense and relax major muscle groups in a sequence," reports Dr. Richard Surwit of Duke University Medical Center. "Once someone gets good at this, they become more aware of when their body's stress levels deviate from what they should. They have a very good way of dealing with it."

Some people find stress relief through visualization. This is a relaxation technique that involves imagining, or visualizing, a picture, peaceful setting, or healthy situation. For example, you could picture yourself jogging without a sugar low, or watching a sunset or ocean waves lapping on a sandy beach. These pictures create an image of your body in a relaxed, balanced, and healthy state. You reinforce the message that your body is strong and can heal itself. People who practice visualization regularly report the technique helps them maintain a sense of calm and well-being. In turn, the calm helps control diabetes by reducing blood pressure and diabetes-related pain.

Many people find meditation produces similar results. With meditation, you focus on your breathing or on a single word or object to reach a relaxed, focused mental state. Studies show that meditation can reduce muscle tension, slow pulse rate, and lower blood pressure.

Yoga provides many of the same benefits. Yoga practice combines deep breathing with physical poses that stretch muscles. Over time, yoga practice builds muscle strength and flexibility. Yoga requires physical and mental control. Therefore, it increases the capacity for the body to do other activities, which eases physical and emotional stress.

Practicing yoga is one way for people with diabetes to relax.

## BIOFEEDBACK

Biofeedback teaches people to become aware of their body's automatic and unconscious processes, such as heart rate and skin temperature. This awareness helps them gain control over the processes. To begin biofeedback, trained personnel connect the patient to a machine that records a specific body function, such as heart rate. The machine relays information about the body's responses as sounds, numbers on a screen, or other visual cues. Gradually, the mind learns to connect these responses with body changes.

Therapists sometimes use biofeedback with other relaxation techniques, such as visualization, to enhance self-awareness. For example, when a biofeedback signal indicates muscle tightening, the patient becomes better able to isolate the problem and use muscle relaxation or another technique to lessen discomfort. Biofeedback provides another tool in the arsenal of stress and pain reducers.

Some people with diabetes who have pain find that acupuncture helps relieve their discomfort.

## ACUPUNCTURE

Acupuncture is widely practiced in China, where the technique began more than five thousand years ago. According to Chinese medicine, a life force known as chi flows like a river through various pathways in the body. As chi circulates, it cleanses and nourishes tissues in different organs. The free flow of chi ensures good health. But an imbalance of chi or a blocked pathway signals ill health, much as a dam backs up a river's flow.

Acupuncture seeks to unblock the dam and correct chi imbalances to restore health. The main focus of acupuncture treatment for diabetes is to relieve chronic pain, such as from nerve damage. Trained acupuncture practitioners insert thin needles at specific points along the pathways. Needles are thought to stimulate the release of the body's natural painkillers. These painkillers relieve pain, which reduces stress.

# CHAPTER EIGHT

# DARK HISTORY, BRIGHTER FUTURE

Jamie, seven, was born with type 1 diabetes. Her parents first learned that their daughter was ill when she was one month old. From then on, the family checked Jamie's blood sugar levels and injected insulin several times a day. Jamie endured constant finger sticks and food monitoring.

This routine lasted for six years. Jamie's world changed after her father heard a doctor talk about a study of children diagnosed with diabetes before six months of age. Researchers at Peninsula Medical School in Great Britain found that some newborns showed changes in one of two key genes involving insulin-producing beta cells. If Jamie was one of those rare children, her diabetes might respond to medication.

Jamie's saliva was tested for the genetic changes, and results showed a match. Her altered genes reduced her body's ability to produce insulin. This finding turned out to be wonderful news. Jamie's form of diabetes responded to a class of drugs normally used for type 2 diabetes. After a week on this medication, Jamie's body produced insulin for the first time. She still needed to watch what she ate and get her blood tested. But she took pills and her parents tested her blood sugar only twice a day to regulate glucose levels. She no longer needed insulin injections.

## SEARCHING FOR A CURE

Research into diabetes continues to expand what is known about the disease. New discoveries change how people with diabetes live and how long they can manage their condition without experiencing disease-related problems. But this was not always the case. At one time, high blood sugar meant certain death. Doctors had little knowledge about the cause and treatments for diabetes. People with the condition became dehydrated and wasted away. Only recently has medical science advanced enough to allow people with diabetes to live nearly normal lives.

Over the centuries, doctors tried various treatments to keep patients from dying of diabetes. During the 1700s and 1800s, doctors believed that eliminating disease through body fluids was the best way to cure most diseases. So they cut patients' veins to allow blood to drip out in a process known as bloodletting. They gave patients substances to make them vomit or empty their bowels. Some doctors believed that sweating rid the body of disease. They wrapped patients in warm flannel or plaster, or they rubbed the skin with a brush or coarse towel to make the body sweat. When these procedures failed, doctors prescribed strong drugs, such as morphine or opium. None of these treatments reduced the grave effects of diabetes.

During the late 1800s, doctors added restricted diets to diabetes treatment. One program required fasting for several days followed by a limited diet. The meal plan consisted of "plain blood puddings" that mixed fat, blood, and spoiled meat. Other diets permitted only green vegetables or oatmeal, rice, potatoes, or milk. To ensure that patients stuck with these diets, doctors sometimes locked them in a room for days. But the diets failed to save patient lives.

## THE DISCOVERY OF INSULIN

In 1889 German scientists Joseph von Mering and Oskar Minkowski conducted a breakthrough experiment. While investigating digestion of fats, they removed a dog's pancreas. Their experiment

Joseph von Mering *(left)* and Oskar Minkowski *(right)*, both German scientists in the 1800s, were the first to link the pancreas to blood sugar levels in the body.

yielded unexpected results. Within a short time, the dog began to urinate often. The men noticed the dog urine attracted swarms of flies. Curious, the scientists tested the urine and discovered that it contained a large amount of sugar. Mering and Minkowski concluded that substances produced in the pancreas must control sugar levels in the body. This finding linked the pancreas to blood sugar levels and diabetes.

Many researchers tried to figure out how the pancreas controlled blood sugar. In 1921 a young Canadian doctor, Frederick Banting, and his assistant, Charles Best, removed a dog's pancreas and extracted a substance from the islets of Langerhans. These cells were named for Paul Langerhans, the scientist who had first described them in 1869. The dog's blood sugar levels dropped. Banting then put the extract back into the dog's bloodstream. The injection resulted in blood sugar levels returning to normal and sugar-free urine.

Banting worked under the supervision of Professor John Macleod, who was thrilled with the results. Macleod thought the extract was a hormone, which he named insulin. Macleod encouraged Banting to perform more studies. After several successful trials with dogs, Banting experimented with injecting insulin into humans with diabetes. The insulin he used for these patients came from cow pancreases.

Banting's first injection into a fourteen-year-old boy with diabetes showed little promise. Macleod worked with biochemist J. B. Collip on better ways to extract the hormone from cows and purify it for human use. The cleaner insulin achieved success. Within two weeks, the boy, who originally weighed only 65 pounds (29 kg), gained weight and looked stronger. He continued to thrive for the next fifteen years, as long as he received insulin injections.

News of this breakthrough treatment rocked the medical community. Within a year, large-scale production of insulin from

Dr. Frederick Banting and his assistant, Charles Best, pose around 1922 with one of the dogs from their experiments.

cows and pigs began. Newspapers and professional journals heralded daily insulin injections as a cure for diabetes. In 1923 Banting and Mcleod received the Nobel Prize in Medicine for the discovery and development of insulin. Banting shared his prize with Best, and Mcleod shared his with Collip.

## NEW HOPE

The discovery of insulin in 1921 brought new hope and the promise of longer lives for people with diabetes. But the ups and downs of managing insulin and diet continued to pose challenges. Some patients suffered reactions to injections made from animal insulin. They experienced pitted skin, rashes, welts, and other unpleasant side effects.

As doctors learned more about diabetes, they noticed that the disease triggered other problems besides extreme sugar levels. They discovered that diabetes damaged the heart, the nervous system, kidneys, and eyes. Researchers continued to look for ways to refine treatment and reduce complications.

During the 1930s, chemists created a longer-acting form of insulin. The idea of shorter- and longer-acting insulin offered the possibility of tighter control of sugar levels. About twenty years later, the first oral medications for people with type 2 diabetes became available.

In 1958 Canadian physician Frederick Sanger separated cow insulin into its simplest components. His discovery paved the way for insulin to be chemically engineered to mirror what humans produce naturally. In recent years, manufacturers developed several new forms of insulin from bacteria found in humans, rather than animals. These different medications benefited people with diabetes who also had animal allergies.

In the 1950s, Frederick Sanger, a Canadian doctor, was the first to separate insulin into its different parts. This led to scientists being able to chemically engineer insulin.

Along with new forms of insulin and medications, manufacturers developed better needles, test strips, glucose meters, continuous glucose monitors and insulin pumps. These advances, however, still require self-testing with a meter to verify the accuracy of other devices.

"Six years after I was diagnosed at age twelve, doctors came up with so much research," Melissa says. "When I was diagnosed, we were still doing urine testing to detect sugar. They did not have short-acting insulin. You could not test blood on your own. You had to go to a doctor. The amount of control I can get on my own has changed so much since then."

## THE FUTURE

Medical science has come a long way toward understanding and treating diabetes. Still, the search for a cure is not over. Researchers continue to investigate advances that will make diabetes treatment easier and hopefully cure the disease completely.

Life
SECTION D

December 29, 2008

From the Pages of USA TODAY

# Gastric bypass can reverse type 2 diabetes in teenagers

Weight loss surgery can reverse diabetes in teens, according to a small study released in the journal *Pediatrics*.

Researchers at Cincinnati Children's Hospital Medical Center [in Ohio] and five other medical centers followed 78 teenagers with type 2 diabetes. Eleven of the study participants, ages 13 to 21, had gastric bypass surgery, and the others followed routine management of their diabetes with medicine and lifestyle modifications.

All 11 teens who had surgery were at least 100 pounds [45 kg] over the ideal weight for their age and build before the procedure. Within a year after surgery, all but one had dropped about one-third of their body weight and had stopped taking medication for type 2 diabetes. The patients came off all diabetic medications, returned to normal blood glucose and insulin levels and significantly improved their blood pressure and cholesterol. Patients who did not have surgery experienced limited health changes for the better.

Surgery could offer a solution for seriously overweight teens who do not respond to the arsenal of other diabetes treatments— those at highest risk for kidney disease, serious vision problems and nerve damage as early as their 20s and 30s.

*—Mary Brophy Marcus*

## USA TODAY Snapshots®

### A boom in surgery for obesity

The number of people getting bariatric surgery, which includes gastric bypass, has risen more than 800% since 1998:

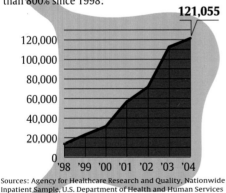

121,055

Sources: Agency for Healthcare Research and Quality, Nationwide Inpatient Sample, U.S. Department of Health and Human Services

By Tracey Wong Briggs and Sam Ward, USA TODAY, 2007

## BREAKING THE GENE CODE

In 2002 scientists in Boston, Massachusetts, discovered a third gene related to type 1 diabetes. They believed the three genes work as a team to control insulin production in beta cells. If any of these genes is faulty or missing, the pancreas cannot manufacture insulin. In 2007 researchers identified other genes that increase the likelihood that a person would develop type 2 diabetes. Scientists discovered that these genes, located on three different chromosomes, explain much of the inherited tendency to acquire type 2 diabetes. Today, researchers have linked eight genes to type 2 diabetes and are studying others. The latest discovery focuses on a connection between genes that influence weight and how body weight increases the risk of acquiring type 2 diabetes.

Understanding the genetics of diabetes helps scientists produce tests to screen for diabetes before it develops. This understanding may also help researchers create new, healthy replacement genes from stem cells. Most body cells carry codes that tell them to mature

Stem cell research, such as this experiment at a laboratory in Germany, may lead to replacement genes for genes that cause diabetes.

into a particular type of cell. But stem cells are unprogrammed. They possess the ability to grow into any type of cell or organ, including beta cells in the pancreas. Stem cells hold great promise to replace damaged beta cells. But scientists are still working to understand how to program these cells into beta cells.

## TRANSPLANTS

Damaged organs may be replaced with healthy ones through transplant surgery. Some people with type 1 diabetes and severe complications choose a pancreas transplant. A healthy pancreas comes from a donor who has just died or a living relative can offer a partial pancreas. But transplant surgery comes with decisions to weigh. The surgery poses risks for both patients, because any surgery is dangerous. What's more, the immune system in the person with diabetes may reject and attack the new pancreas. Transplant patients usually need medications to help curb rejection. But these drugs are costly, and they often cause other health problems.

Another type of transplant uses islet cells from a donor pancreas. Transplanting islet cells may help people with diabetes someday, but this surgery is still experimental. So far, the surgery involves some of the same problems as pancreas transplants. Researchers are investigating less dangerous antirejection medication and improved surgery techniques. One avenue of research explores a coating to protect transplanted islet cells from attack by the immune system. Another approach investigates creating artificial islet cells that can be implanted elsewhere in the body but will produce insulin whenever blood sugar levels rise.

## IMMUNE THERAPY

Researchers are using a technique called targeted antibodies to extend the honeymoon phase of type 1 diabetes and preserve the

## Did You Know?

Certain foods may help bring the body back into balance. Although more research is needed, these foods show promise for some people in reducing signs of diabetes.

- Cinnamon (1 teaspoon per day) helps regulate blood sugar levels.
- Peanut butter (1 tablespoon) helps sugar levels stay balanced longer, especially when added to morning oatmeal.
- Cayenne pepper burns sugar in blood, reduces inflammation, and helps the body lose heat through the skin, which contributes to weight loss.
- Blueberry leaves boiled into tea helps lower blood sugar levels.
- Huckleberries and mulberries (enough to cover morning cereal each day) bring sugar levels down.
- Coffee (four cups per day) has been linked to reduced risk of type 2 diabetes in rats by enhancing the liver's capacity to reduce sugar levels.

function of insulin-producing beta cells. These special antibodies latch onto a type of immune system cell that attacks beta cells in the pancreas. At first the patient's immune system cell counts drop. But when the antibodies multiply several weeks later, new immune system cells attack the beta cells in a different way. They seem reprogrammed. The effect might help preserve beta cell function for a year or longer. Research into this type of treatment is still in the experimental phase.

## IMPLANTED MONITORS

In addition to a cure, scientists are also investigating better ways to help patients control blood sugar levels. One goal is to "close the loop." This phrase refers to an all-in-one device that monitors blood sugar levels and automatically releases insulin when needed. Various versions of such devices have been developed already, but researchers constantly work to improve them. One version is surgically implanted in the body. Another stays outside the body but has a tube that goes through the skin. Both versions are being tested to see if they function as predicted and whether patients find them easier to use than those already on the market.

## DRUG PREVENTION

Diabetes is a complicated disease. And complications from uncontrolled blood sugar are expensive to manage and treat. That's why some drug manufacturers are concentrating on developing medications to prevent diabetes in millions of people at high risk for the disease. So far, studies of one new drug indicated that people in this category reduced their chance of developing diabetes by two-thirds. But other tests of the same drug proved mixed, so government approval is a long way off.

Other classes of drugs focus on reducing specific diseases common in people with diabetes. Different drugs lower blood pressure or reduce heart disease in people with diabetes. But these drugs, too, have come under fire for serious side effects. Drug companies hope to improve results for patients that need constant observation by doctors to prevent other problems.

Rising numbers of diabetes cases cause great concern for the health-care community. Government agencies, scientists, and manufacturers are investing time and money to find better ways to prevent and treat the disease. In the meantime, people with diabetes

March 22, 2010

From the Pages of USA TODAY

# Study urges vitamin D supplement for infants: Mothers often deficient, too.

Most babies should take a daily vitamin D supplement, a new study shows. Only 1 to 13 percent of infants under one year now get a vitamin D supplement, available in inexpensive drops, according to a study published online in *Pediatrics*. Those drops are needed, the study says, because only 5 to 37 percent of American infants met the standard for vitamin D: 400 international units a day.

Vitamin D strengthens bone and the immune system and also appears to prevent type 1 diabetes, heart disease, and cancer, the paper says.

A second study in *Pediatrics* reports that 58 percent of newborns and 36 percent of mothers were deficient in vitamin D, according to blood tests. Although taking prenatal vitamins helped, more that 30 percent of moms who took them were still deficient. Getting lots of sunlight helped raise vitamin D levels in moms, but not in their newborns.

—Liz Szabo

are learning more about how to help themselves. "I try to plug diabetes into the natural way I think of the world," Jared explains. "You get what you put into what you do. If you're lazy and stupid about your care, you're going to have troubles. If you're vigilant, you'll have a successful life."

# GLOSSARY

**acupuncture:** an ancient Chinese medical practice that uses thin needles inserted along nerve pathways to relieve pain and treat disease

**Alzheimer's disease:** a brain disease characterized by protein plaques that interfere with transmission of messages, resulting in memory loss

**amyloid:** a destructive protein that may be involved in diabetes and Alzheimer's disease

**antibodies:** immune system units made of protein molecules that recognize, destroy, and remember invading microbes, such as bacteria and viruses

**arteries:** vessels that carry blood from the heart to all tissues and organs in the body

**autoantibodies:** immune system protein molecules that wrongly identify "foreign" substances and attack the body's own healthy cells

**autoimmune diseases:** diseases that occur when someone's immune system attacks his or her own tissues and cells

**beta cells:** cells in areas of the pancreas called islets. Beta cells make and release insulin, a hormone that controls the level of glucose (sugar) in the blood.

**biofeedback:** a technique to reduce stress and pain by learning to recognize and control changes in automatic body processes, such as heart rate

**blood glucose:** the amount of sugar (glucose) in the blood at a given time

**blood pressure:** the force of blood against artery walls. High blood pressure contributes to heart disease.

**blood sugar:** an informal name for blood glucose

**blood sugar meter:** a device for testing how much glucose (sugar) is in the blood at one point in time

**carbohydrates:** one of the three major components of food, along with protein and fats. Carbohydrates supply the body's main source of energy.

**chromosomes:** rod-shaped structures within cells that contain genes, the basic units of heredity

**complex carbohydrates:** carbohydrates that come from sugars in whole-grain products, dried peas and beans, legumes, and starchy vegetables, such as potatoes and corn

**continuous glucose monitor (CGM):** a device made up of a sensor, which collects blood sugar readings from interstitial fluid under the skin and a small monitor, which records the readings. Readings are taken approximately every five minutes, or 288 times every twenty-four hours.

**dehydration:** abnormal and excessive loss of body fluids

**diabetes:** a disease, also known as diabetes mellitus, that occurs when the body is unable to use sugar properly, resulting in high levels of blood sugar

**dietitians:** nutrition specialists who help plan healthy food choices and meals. A registered dietitian (RD) has special training.

**digestion:** the process whereby the body breaks down food into smaller particles to be used for fuel and nutrition

**endocrine system:** the glands and organs that produce hormones and release them into the bloodstream to help operate body processes, including metabolism (use of food for energy), growth, and sexual function

**endocrinologist:** a medical doctor trained to diagnose and treat disorders of the endocrine system

**fasting plasma glucose test:** a test for diabetes that measures glucose levels in blood plasma after a person has fasted (not eaten) for eight hours

**fiber:** an indigestible substance found in foods that come from plants, including whole-grain products, fruits, and vegetables. Fiber is part of a healthy diet.

**genes:** chemical units in cells that contain coded instructions for forming proteins. Genes determine traits that are passed from parent to child.

**gestational diabetes:** a form of diabetes that develops during pregnancy

**glucagon:** a hormone that prompts the liver to convert glycogen into glucose and release it into the bloodstream. An injection of glucagon is used to revive someone who has lost consciousness due to hypoglycemia.

**glucose:** a type of sugar that the body makes from the elements of food—proteins, fats, and carbohydrates. Glucose comes mostly from carbohydrates and is the main source of fuel for growth and activity. Glucose cannot enter body cells without the help of insulin, which acts as a key or gatekeeper.

**glucose tolerance test:** a test for diabetes that shows blood sugar levels over time after a person drinks a sugary liquid

**glycogen:** sugar stored in the liver that is released when blood sugar levels drop too low and the body needs energy

**hormones:** chemicals produced in cells that travel in body fluids and stimulate other cells to do their job

**hyperglycemia:** high blood sugar

**hypoglycemia:** low blood sugar

**immune system:** the units of the body that work together to fight disease

**injections:** the use of a needle and syringe or pen to put liquid into the body

**insulin:** a hormone produced in the pancreas that acts as a gatekeeper to allow sugar to pass into cells

**insulin pump:** a device that delivers a continuous supply of rapid-acting insulin into the body through a thin, flexible plastic tube that is inserted into the skin

**insulin resistance:** a condition common in people with type 2 diabetes in which the body does not respond to insulin

**interstitial fluid:** clear fluid under the skin that carries glucose and other nutrients from the bloodstream to the cells

**islets:** clumps, or islands, of cells, also known as islets of Langerhans, found in the pancreas. Islets hold beta cells, which produce insulin.

**ketoacidosis:** a severe, life-threatening disorder, also called diabetic ketoacidosis (DKA), caused by a lack of circulating insulin. The body uses stored fat for fuel, which results in production of toxic fatty acids called ketones.

**ketones:** fatty acids produced from the breakdown of fat for fuel

**lancet:** a sharp, fine needle that pricks the skin to draw blood for glucose testing

**meditation:** a form of relaxation that involves focusing on the breath, a word, or an object

**metabolism:** the way the body chemically changes food into the nutrients and energy needed to sustain life

**nephropathy:** kidney disease

**neuropathy:** nerve damage

**pancreas:** a small organ that lies behind the lower part of the stomach. As part of the endocrine system, the pancreas makes insulin and digestive enzymes.

**plasma:** the liquid part of blood

**prediabetes:** borderline high blood sugar levels, which indicate an increased risk of developing diabetes

**retinopathy:** damage to small blood vessels in the back of the eye (retina) that causes blurred vision and other vision problems

**simple carbohydrates:** carbohydrates that come from sugars, such as table sugar, processed flour, candy, soda, and snack foods

**stem cells:** primary cells that can become any type of cell. Researchers are investigating use of stem cells to replace damaged beta cells in the pancreas.

**type 1 diabetes:** a disease, most often diagnosed in children and young adults, in which the body produces little or no insulin

**type 2 diabetes:** the most common form of diabetes in which the body either does not produce enough insulin or does not use insulin properly. Type 2 typically affects middle-aged and older people, but younger adults and children can get it too.

**visualization:** a technique to reduce stress and pain by picturing a healthy body or relaxed setting

**yoga:** a body-mind practice that combines deep breathing with physical poses

# RESOURCES

**American Diabetes Association**
**1701 North Beauregard Street**
**Alexandria, VA 22311**
**(800) DIABETES (342-2383)**
**http://www.diabetes.org**

This national organization offers online and printed information about diabetes, local programs and resources, such as finding diabetes educators, and an online questionnaire that calculates an individual's risk of acquiring diabetes.

**Diabetes Exercise and Sports Association**
**8001 Montcastle Drive**
**Nashville, TN 37221**
**(800) 898-4322**
**http://www.diabetes-exercise.org**

This national organization, with local chapters and a newsletter, connects people with diabetes who enjoy healthy and safe exercise.

**Juvenile Diabetes Research Foundation International**
**26 Broadway**
**New York, NY 10004**
**(800) 533-2873**
**http://www.jdrf.org**

This international organization focuses on type 1 diabetes and raises funds, sponsors clinical research trials, runs diabetes camps, and publishes *Teen Countdown* magazine and *Kids Online* (http://kids.jdrf.org) and *Life with Diabetes* e-newsletters.

**National Diabetes Education Program**
**One Diabetes Way**
**Bethesda, MD 20814-9692**
**(800) 438-5383**
**http://www.ndep.nih.gov**

This general information site offers online brochures and access to current diabetes studies.

**National Diabetes Information Clearinghouse**
**1 Information Way**
**Bethesda, MD 20892-3560**
**(800) 860-8747**
**http://diabetes.niddk.nih.gov/**

This site, part of the U.S. government's National Institute of Diabetes and Digestive and Kidney Diseases, offers downloadable and printed brochures on a range of topics affecting people with diabetes.

**TCOYD—Taking Control of Your Diabetes**
**1110 Camino Del Mar, Suite B**
**Del Mar, CA 92014**
**(800) 99-TCOYD (82693)**
**http://www.tcoyd.org**

This organization produces conferences and health fairs for people with diabetes and their families, quarterly newsletters, and a television series about different diabetes-related topics.

# SOURCE NOTES

5    Chris Feudtner, *Bittersweet: Diabetes, Insulin, and the Transformation of Illness* (Chapel Hill: University of North Carolina Press, 2003), 4.

5    Ibid., 4, 224.

5    Ibid., 5.

9    Jared, personal interview with author, Chicago, IL, June 16, 2006.

12    Reuters, "Diabetes Rate Doubled in Last 30 Years," *CNN.com*. (June 22, 2006)

13    Carl, personal interview with author, Noblesville, IN, June 15, 2006.

24    Marc Santora, "East Meets West, Adding Pounds and Peril," *New York Times*, January 12, 2006, 1A.

35    Jared, personal interview.

36    Christine Potema, ed., *JDRF Illinois News*, Fall 2006, 6.

38    Ann, personal interview with author, Evanston, IL, June 13, 2006.

45    Emily, personal interview with author, Chicago, IL, May 30, 2006.

51    Jared, personal interview.

52    Richard Bernstein, *Dr. Bernstein's Diabetes Solution: The Complete Guide to Achieving Normal Blood Sugars* (Boston: Little, Brown and Co., 2003), 205.

57    Bob, personal interview with author, Wilmette, IL, June 28, 2006.

58    Emily, personal interview.

58    Ibid.

62    Alex Berenson, "A Ray of Hope for Diabetics," *New York Times*, March 2, 2006, C4.

65    Jared, personal interview.

67    Melissa, personal interview, Northbrook, IL, July 11, 2006.

70    Jared, personal interview.

71    Emily, personal interview.

72    Jared, personal interview.

73    Mary Brophy Marcus, "Diabetics with Heart Disease: Meds vs. Surgery," *USA Today*, June 8, 2009, D4.

78  Rebecca Lanning, ed., *American Diabetes Association Complete Guide to Diabetes*, 4th ed. (Alexandria, VA: American Diabetes Association, 2005), 311.

84  Melissa, personal interview with author, Northbrook, IL, July 11, 2006.

87  Ann, personal interview.

88  Ibid.

90  Melissa, personal interview.

93  Emily, personal interview.

93  Carl, personal interview.

94  Tracey Koepke, "Stress Management as a Factor in Healthy Living," *DukeMedNews*, January 18, 2002, http://www.dukemednews.org/av/medminute.php?id-5268 (June 20, 2007).

94  Jared, personal interview.

96–97  Koepke, "Stress Management."

101  Canadian Diabetes Association, "The History of Diabetes," 2007, http://www.diabetes.ca/section_About/timeline.asp (June 20, 2007).

105  Melissa, personal interview.

110  Paula Ford-Martin, *The Everything Diabetes Book* (Avon, MA: Adams Media, 2004), 290.

111  Jared, personal interview.

# SELECTED BIBLIOGRAPHY

Bernstein, Richard. *Dr. Bernstein's Diabetes Solution: The Complete Guide to Achieving Normal Blood Sugars*. Boston: Little, Brown and Co., 2003.

Center for Nutrition Policy and Promotion. "How Much Are You Eating?" Washington, DC: United States Department of Agriculture, 2002.

Centers for Disease Control and Prevention, National Health and Nutrition Examination Survey. *National Diabetes Fact Sheet*, 2005. Atlanta: U.S. Department of Health and Human Services, 2005.

Collazo-Clavell, Maria, ed. *Mayo Clinic on Managing Diabetes*. Rochester, MN: Mayo Clinic, 2001.

Dragisic, Patricia, ed. *The American Medical Association Complete Medical Encyclopedia*. New York: Random House, 2003.

Feudtner, Chris. *Bittersweet: Diabetes, Insulin, and the Transformation of Illness*. Chapel Hill: University of North Carolina Press, 2003.

Ford-Martin, Paula. *The Everything Diabetes Book*. Avon, MA: Adams Media, 2004.

Gehling, Eve. *The Family & Friends' Guide to Diabetes*. New York: John Wiley & Sons, 2000.

Grady, Denise. "Link between Diabetes and Alzheimer's Disease." *New York Times*, July 17, 2006, A15.

Guthrie, Diana. *The Diabetes Sourcebook*. New York: McGraw-Hill, 2004.

JDRF. "Diabetes Complications." Juvenile Diabetes Research Foundation International. December 15, 2006. http://www.jdrf.org/index.cfm?page_id=101308 (June 21, 2007).

Lanning, Rebecca, ed. *American Diabetes Association Complete Guide to Diabetes*. 4th ed. Alexandria, VA: American Diabetes Association, 2005.

LifeMed Media, "Blood Glucose Monitoring." dLife. August 29, 2006. http://www.dlife.com/dLife/do/ShowContent/blood_sugar_management/testing/ (June 21, 2007).

National Diabetes Information Clearinghouse. *Diabetes Overview*. U. S. Department of Health and Human Services. NIH Publication 06-3875, April 2006.

Rosenthal, Elisabeth. "Drug Can Prevent Diabetes in Many at High Risk, Study Suggests." *International Herald Tribune*, September 17, 2006. http://www.nytimes .com/2006/09/17/world/17diabetes.html (June 20, 2007).

Santora, Marc. "Concern Grows over Increase in Diabetes around World." *New York Times*, June 11, 2006.

WHO. "Welcome to the Diabetes Programme," World Health Organization, 2007. http://www.who.int/diabetes/en (June 20, 2007).

# FURTHER READING AND WEBSITES

**Books**

Barrier, Phyllis. *Type 2 Diabetes for Beginners*. Alexandria, VA: American Diabetes Association, 2005.

Becker. Gretchen. *The First Year: Type 2 Diabetes; An Essential Guide for the Newly Diagnosed*. 2nd ed. Cambridge, MA: Da Capo Press, 2006.

Edelman, Steven V. *Taking Control of Your Diabetes*. 3rd ed. Caddo, OK: Professional Communications, 2007.

Garnero, Theresa. *Your First Year with Diabetes*. Alexandria, VA: American Diabetes Association, 2008.

Geil. Patti. *What Do I Eat Now?* Alexandria, VA: American Diabetes Association, 2009.

Gray, Shirley Wimbish. *Living with Diabetes*. Chanhassen, MN: Child's World, 2003.

Loy, Bo. *487 Really Cool Tips for Kids with Diabetes*. Alexandria, VA: American Diabetes Association, 2004.

Ruhl, Jenny. *Blood Sugar 101: What They Don't Tell You about Diabetes*. Turner Falls, MA: Technion Books, 2009.

U.S. Department of Health and Human Services. *Keep the Beat: Heart Healthy Recipes*. National Institutes of Health, National Heart, Lung, and Blood Institute, NIH Publication No. 03-2921. 2003. Available online at http://www.nhlbi.nih.gov/health/public/heart/other/ktb_recipebk/ktb_recipebk.pdf (February 1, 2011).

Expand learning beyond the printed book. Download free, complementary educational resources for this book from our website, www.lerneresource.com

## Websites

The ADA Wizdom Youth Zone
**http://www.diabetes.org/wizdom**

The American Diabetes Association (ADA) site offers fun information kits for kids.

American Dietetic Association
**http://www.eatright.org**

The American Dietetic Association is the world's largest organization devoted to food and nutrition, offering meal-planning information for people with diabetes.

Children with Diabetes
**http://www.childrenwithdiabetes.com**

This site offers resources and chat rooms for kids with diabetes and their families.

Diabetes Camping Association
**http://www.diabetescamp.org**

This agency focuses on camps for children with diabetes.

Mayo Clinic
**http://www.mayoclinic.com/health/diabetes/DS01121**

Mayo Clinic is a respected medical institution with doctors who use the latest diagnostic and treatments methods in dealing with patients who have diabetes.

National Institutes of Health National Center for Complementary and Alternative Medicine
**http://nccam.nih.gov**

This site links readers to the latest research studies that investigate alternative diabetes treatments.

# INDEX

# ABOUT THE AUTHOR

Marlene Targ Brill is an award-winning author of sixty-five books. She especially likes to write about ways to help readers feel better and understand how their bodies function. As a young student, she enjoyed learning about the body and wanted to work in medicine. Instead, she became a teacher of children with special needs. She writes about a variety of topics, especially in the health-care field, including Alzheimer's disease, Down syndrome, and autism.

# PHOTO ACKNOWLEDGMENTS